"Adults have a unique opportunity and responsibi
wonderful each of them is. Letters can be powerf
they receive a letter, and its message can be read
Incredible Kid Day reminds us all of the power of t..........

— **Dr. Frank Farley,** *professor, Temple University;*
past president, American Psychological Association

"Time and time again as a professional counselor, I have seen the huge, positive impact this
kind of communication has in a young person's life. It does make a difference."

— **Dr. Gregory Jantz,** *counselor; speaker; author,*
Becoming Strong Again: How to Regain Emotional Health

"Writing a letter for *Absolutely Incredible Kid Day* can light a fire in a child that
will warm both your hearts."

— **Carole Lieberman, M.D., Ph.D.,**
talk show host; on-air personality

"*Absolutely Incredible Kid Day* gives children and adults an opportunity to share important
thoughts and feelings. Children should be told they are loved and appreciated in as many
ways as possible, and writing these sentiments can be as beneficial to adults as it is
for children."

— **Pat Baxter,** *licensed therapist;*
co-author, An Owner's Guide to Parenting Teenagers

"A genuine, thoughtful letter from a parent can provide important emotional support to
a child. I hope everyone will take the time to write to a child on *Absolutely Incredible
Kid Day*. It's an easy way to say you care a lot."

— **Barbara Berg,** *clinical social worker;*
author, What To Do When Life Is Driving You Crazy

"I write letters, cards, etc., to my kids and nieces and nephews all the time. It helps us get
to know each other. It sets a good example and shows kids how to care for others."

— **Lisa Marie Nelson, Ph.D.,** *broadcast journalist;*
co-author, The Healthy Family Handbook

"Given the tremendous challenges and threats facing our children today, connecting caring
adults and young people is more important than ever. The Partnership for Children and
I support the efforts of Camp Fire Boys and Girls to make such connections through
Absolutely Incredible Kid Day. Take the time to tell a youngster that you care about him
or her. This is good for the children!"

— **Jim Caccamo, Ph.D.,** *executive director,*
The Partnership for Children

"What a great idea. Often in the hustle and bustle of everyday life, we forget to mention the strengths we see in our children. Focusing on the positive helps them develop self-confidence and courage."

— **Marilyn Gootman,** *author, When a Friend Dies: A Book for Teens about Grieving and Healing*

"Participating in *Absolutely Incredible Kid Day* provides rewards for everyone. It teaches children that someone cares and sets an example for how they can care for others; it teaches adults that writing can be a useful tool to understand one's inner emotions; and it teaches everyone the value of supporting each other throughout life."

— **Dr. Muriel S. Savikas,** *founder, parenting101.com; author, Guilt is Good: What Working Moms Need to Know*

"Writing letters to young people is a wonderful way of affirming their self-worth, for it demonstrates to them that they are noticed, cared about and special. And because letters allow for a more thoughtful and detailed expression of ideas and feelings, it is an invaluable tool for communicating the unspoken. Finally, because letters can be read and reread, their words of encouragement and appreciation can sustain a child for years to come."

— **Susan Maxwell,** *licensed family therapist; speaker; media commentator*

"Many kids today are starved for adults who treat them with respect, kindness and honesty. Letter writing is a perfect vehicle for adults who wish to nurture, encourage and mentor young people. The privacy afforded to sender and recipient by letter writing offers advantages over verbal communication in that it makes it easier to "say" and "hear" deeply felt sentiments of love and affection."

— **Alex J. Packer, Ph.D.,** *president, FCD Educational Services, Inc.; author, How Rude! The Teenagers' Guide to Good Manners, Proper Behavior, and Not Grossing People Out*

"It's a very creative idea. Kids will be touched, and they will feel wanted. It's a great way to help them grow up to be thinking, feeling human beings who will care about themselves and others."

— **Dr. Myrna B. Shure,** *author, Raising a Thinking Preteen*

"I remember getting letters, as a very little girl, from an uncle who was stationed overseas during World War II. Here he was, fighting a war, and he took the time to write to us kids. We felt loved, honored and important because he thought we were worthy of his time. To this day, the value of those letters to my self-image is immeasurable."

— **Taube S. Kaufman,** *specialist in family relationships; author, The Combined Family: A Guide to Creating Successful Step-relationships*

Letters
FROM THE
Heart

A CelebRation of LeTters to AbsolutelY IncreDiBle KiDS!

Edited by Stewart Smith
National Executive Director, Camp Fire Boys and Girls

Foreword by Jim Fay
Co-Author of *Parenting With Love and Logic*

Camp Fire Press

4601 Madison Avenue, Kansas City, MO 64112

LETTERS FROM THE HEART.

Published by Camp Fire Press, 4601 Madison Avenue, Kansas City, Missouri 64112.
First edition. ISBN: 0-9674529-0-2

First paperback printing, 2000.

Letters from the heart : a celebration of letters to
    absolutely incredible kids! / edited by Stewart
    Smith. -- 1st ed.
       p. cm.
       ISBN: 0-9674529-0-2

    1. Parents--Correspondence. 2. Parent and
    child. 3. Letter writing. I. Smith, Stewart.

    HQ755.85.L48 2000   306.874
                       QBI99-1487
COVER DESIGN by Molly Alspaugh/Fleishman-Hillard Kansas City Design Group
COVER PHOTO by Mark McDonald
Children featured on the cover are: (l. to r.)
Taylor Briggs-Whitaker, Erica Gonzales, Mackenzie Ortego.

ACKNOWLEDGEMENTS:

I owe sincere appreciation to the moms, dads,
aunts, uncles, grandparents, mentors, volunteers
and celebrities who shared a letter and touched
the child in all of us. You are the heroes of this book.

To Camp Fire Boys and Girls' councils across the
United States, I thank you for your dedication and
care in realizing Camp Fire's mission of building caring,
confident youth and future leaders. You took the vision
of *Absolutely Incredible Kid Day* and developed it
into a living, breathing gift to our children and youth.

To the judges, I express my gratitude for your heartfelt
review and assistance in selecting the letters for
publication. As a fellow judge, I know you also
saw love expressed on every page of every letter.
Thanks to Andrew Carroll; Gregory Jantz, Ph.D.;
Frank Farley, Ph.D.; Lisa Marie Nelson, Ph.D.;
and Paul Anderson, Ph.D.

DEDICATED TO: Camp Fire's National Youth Advisory Cabinet.
You are my inspiration.

A Letter From Stewart Smith, National Executive Director, Camp Fire Boys and Girls

n today's marathon-paced world, many traditions seem outdated. Sweet but old-fashioned rituals appear to be out-of-step with the way we live now. Neighbors don't talk much anymore. When they do speak, it's more likely the result of a chance meeting at the video store than an intentional encounter. We bank using an ATM; there's no need to rely on a teller. And writing a letter is almost unheard of. Why would you, when phones are faster and within easy reach, thank you very much.

It strikes me that we're missing something by living at this pace, particularly when it comes to letter writing. You see, a letter is so much more than a way to communicate. A thoughtfully worded letter, especially one that's handwritten, contains a little of the author's heart and soul. And, for the receiver, the letter is a tangible expression of love or commitment, a memento that can be treasured for a lifetime.

It's in that spirit that Camp Fire Boys and Girls created *Absolutely Incredible Kid Day*, celebrated on the third Thursday of each March. What is Kid Day? It's an annual call to action, a reminder to all adults that they can make a world of difference in a child's life by telling that child, in writing, how much he or she is loved and cherished. It's a simple gesture, costing nothing more than the 10 minutes it takes to compose the letter. But the rewards to writer and receiver alike are rich and long-lasting.

This book proves that point. Since the debut of *Absolutely Incredible Kid Day* in March 1997, adults have written hundreds of thousands of letters to the kids in their lives. Sometimes adults write letters to kids outside their own families, to a child down the block, a young person in foster care or other children in the community who deserve to know they're special.

Here, you'll find some of the most heartwarming examples of the letters Kid Day has inspired. Some of the letters are short; others are lengthy. A few celebrate a child's courage in the face of adversity; most simply communicate the message, "I love you." Length is not important. The point is to create a permanent record of how you feel, a message that survives spoken words or material items you'll give to a child.

Writing a letter is easier than you think! Here are a few tips to make your *Absolutely Incredible Kid Day* experience a memorable one. Keep your letter simple. Often, the words we write are very similar to the encouraging words we might say to kids. The difference is that the letter has permanence. Be specific. Tell the child what makes him or her absolutely incredible. Be positive! There's a time to coach kids and a time to affirm. This is the time to tell them they are loved because of who they are.

After reading letters from other adults and celebrities, you'll find a letter-writing kit in the back of the book. We've even excuse-proofed this book by providing you with stationery.

No learning is so compelling as the one gained by personal experience. Several weeks after the first *Absolutely Incredible Kid Day*, I discovered a letter I received from my father when I was 14 years old. In the same box, I found two notes written by my maternal grandmother after I left for graduate school. My parents and grandparents have been dead for many years now. But my otherwise sketchy memories of my father and grandmother are now robust, alive with color, clarity and an honesty of spirit that only a handwritten letter can evoke.

Give the absolutely incredible kids in your life a similar moment of joy. Write a letter to a child in your life, whether the child you're writing to is 5 or 55.

The 10 minutes you spend writing a letter may be the best investment you make all year long.

Stewart Smith

STEWART SMITH
Editor, *Letters from the Heart*
National Executive Director,
Camp Fire Boys and Girls

TABLE OF CONTENTS:

LETTERS FROM THE HEART

Introduction

or years, I thought I knew how it felt to get a personal letter. I have actually received thousands of them over the last 25 years. Many of these letters are handwritten and countless of these bear the misspellings, slips of the pen, crossed-out words, grammatical errors, and even evidence of the tears that flowed while they were being written. All of these are the unique parts of the letters that make them so absolutely priceless.

Each time I return from my speaking engagements, I hurry into my office, shut the door and read the letters that came while I was gone. These letters usually are expressions of gratitude for lives changed as a result of my work. Make no mistake, I also get the ones that tell how awful I am for making some blunder or expressing a politically incorrect idea that temporarily ruined someone's life. But the vast majority of letters expressing thanks make my heart sing and provide the fuel to keep me motivated to write more books and give more speeches.

I always thought I knew how great it felt to receive a letter. And then one day … boom! Out of the blue, when I least expected it, I got a jolt that lifted me to an entirely new level of understanding.

Some time ago, Shirley, my wonderful wife of 43 years, dragged me down into the basement to categorize our family pictures. "We are going to get all of this organized so that when we pass on, the kids won't have a mess on their hands," she said.

It didn't take me long to see that we had a monumental job on our hands. We were not only going to organize the pictures that came out of our immediate family, but those of our parents' families, as well.

In a short time, she pulled out a very old and tired baby book. "Where did this come from?" I asked. It was one I had never seen in my entire 63 years of life, and what I found put an end to the rest of the day's organizing activities.

I was amazed! I was holding a baby book entitled, "Baby Jimmy 1934." I wondered how I could have gone through all these years not knowing that I had a baby book. The book was tattered, worn and dirty. The stains and worn spots let me know my mother had carried it with her every day, making entries about my growth and progress. I could feel her love right through the dirty, ragged cover.

Better yet, when I opened the book, out fell a tiny letter, folded several times. The paper was brittle and yellowed by the ravages of time. But this letter was the most beautiful thing I had ever seen.

Dear Jimmy,
Today is March 9, 1938. It is your fourth birthday, and I am so proud of the wonderful little boy you have become. Life has been very hard for Daddy and me because of the Depression, and we have been very poor. But we have something that makes us richer than if we had all the money in the world, and that is you. Every morning you wake up with a smile and you run to look out the windows for the birdies. You are a very happy little boy and that makes us happy, too. I am especially proud about how nice you are to the other kids who come to play with you. I know that you will grow up to be a great man some day. Thank you for coming into our lives.

Love, Mom

From the moment I discovered that letter, I could genuinely feel what it's like for a kid to receive a letter from a loved one. It is all the more significant to me because it is the only letter I ever received from my parents. I discovered it when I was 63 years old. It had been hiding all this time, folded inside a book that I didn't even know existed.

Please don't get the wrong impression about my parents. They were very good, very kind people. They just didn't know how incredibly important and rewarding it is for a kid to receive a letter. I'm sure that if Camp Fire Boys and Girls had offered their *Absolutely Incredible Kid Day* back then, encouraging adults to write to their kids, I would not have needed to wait 63 years to feel how a kid's heart sings while reading love letters from a parent. It means all the more to me now that I can share the letter with you. I am proud to be a part of this absolutely incredible and important work.

Happy Reading,

Jim Fay, Ph.D.
Co-author, *Parenting with Love and Logic*

Camp Fire Boys and Girls'
Absolutely Incredible Kid Day

Think back. You're 9 years old.

Your little sister created her artwork on your bed, then pointed at you when your mom found scissor slits and glue on your bedspread. At the soccer play-off game, you slipped and missed a kick that would have won the game, then faked a broken ankle until the coach called your bluff. Mom served creamed spinach over your pork chop at dinner, and Dad said you had to taste it. That night, you were in no mood to come down for s'mores when Mom said she needed to see you smile. You knew you were too old to sleep with Teddy, but it was one of those nights you needed him, so you tucked him under your pillow. He crept out on top of the sheets in the middle of the night, and there was your sister, sucking her thumb in the moonlight, staring at you. She told.

In the morning, you woke up and found a note from your mom. She was the queen of notes, but this one wasn't a list of things to do. You opened it. It started with "I love you," so you held it under the covers in case someone caught you reading a mushy letter. She told you how proud she was that you brought your math grade from a C to a B+ this semester. She told you how worried she was when she thought you'd broken your ankle. She remembered when you scored three goals against the conference champions the month before and how she could hardly stand still next to the coach after that game, because she was about to burst into tears. Her signature, "Mom," was messy. Your fourth-grade teacher would make her rewrite it. That's why you liked it messy, because no one else did things quite like Mom.

You tucked the note under your pillow in case you needed to look at it again. Moms, you figured, are just plain gushy. You got out of bed and thought maybe this morning you could fix her a frozen waffle to give her a good start before she went to work. That one morning, you hugged her back when she gave you her "have a good day" kiss.

A VISION

Camp Fire Boys and Girls wondered what it would be like if every kid in America could receive a letter of encouragement at least once each year. And we wondered what a powerful influence we might have if, on this one day, adults collectively affirmed the goodness and spirit of children through the written word. The change could be absolutely incredible.

We knew letters alone wouldn't end the fear of powerlessness in schools, teen pregnancies or drug abuse, but we were willing to examine the impact a heartfelt message could have on the life of an individual child.

BUILDING A CASE FOR CAMP FIRE'S ABSOLUTELY INCREDIBLE KID DAY

Before launching any program, the policy of Camp Fire Boys and Girls is to conduct in-depth research into how, or even why, it will work. With the help of an experienced researcher, Camp Fire Boys and Girls set out to find how we might encourage parents, aunts and uncles, grandparents and mentors to stop in the middle of their very busy days and write encouraging, loving messages. Our challenge was to create a day that would build self-esteem in kids without sounding hokey or preachy.

We studied parenting values of American ethnic, educational and socioeconomic groups. We looked for trends to see how adults passed along their values, knowledge and traditions to our youth. About the time we compiled our first 3-foot stack of paperwork, we began making notable observations. Authors and psychologists said letter writing was a worthwhile, valuable and enduring way to share thoughts and feelings.

We found that adults were eager to connect with the children in their lives, but that they sometimes struggled to establish those relationships. Grandparents were showing a renewed interest in being involved with their grandchildren. Distinguished child and family experts heartily endorsed *Absolutely Incredible Kid Day*.

"When we offer encouraging words, we fuel the potential for the child's success," said T. Berry Brazelton, M.D., pediatrician and leading child development expert.

Our conclusion? *Absolutely Incredible Kid Day* would become a monumental celebration of children, an intentional opportunity to pass love and affirmation to our nation's youth.

THE INAUGURAL ABSOLUTELY INCREDIBLE KID DAY

In early 1997, after a full year of research and testing, we confidently announced that Camp Fire Boys and Girls would celebrate *Absolutely Incredible Kid Day* annually on the third Thursday in March. With limited resources, we turned to our local councils across the country and to journalists to help us spread the word about this call to action.

We sent news releases, media kits with "Tips for Writing an *Absolutely Incredible Kid Day* Letter," and personal letters to magazines, radio and television programs, and the top 100 daily newspapers and columnists. Our call to America's adults was a simple one: On March 20, 1997, take 20 minutes to write a letter to the child or children in your life and tell them why you love them. In the first year, an estimated 123 million people heard or read about *Absolutely Incredible Kid Day*.

Many of the nation's Fortune 500 companies used *Absolutely Incredible Kid Day* as a way to build employee morale by encouraging them to reinforce the companies' goodwill to their customers and reach out to a child.

Across the nation, adults reported leaving letters on children's pillows, in lunch boxes, and stuck to refrigerators. They mailed the letters in big envelopes, read them over the phone, sent them through e-mail, and some even read them in person. Letters came from grandparents, aunts, uncles, parents, siblings, neighbors, educators, mentors and volunteers. Their supportive words communicated their commitments to the children in our country.

The letters seemed to be as good for adults as they were for the children. Adults said it helped relieve the pressures of long hours away from home to meet the increased demands of their employers. They said letter writing increased intrafamily communication. Step-moms and dads wrote to their kids with such meaningful messages that they allowed their children to stop for an instant and receive or express love. Letters became a small sign that love comes straight from the heart.

WHAT AN IMPACT ... WHAT A FUTURE!

In the following years, *Absolutely Incredible Kid Day* has developed an incredible following. Athletes, politicians, entertainers and celebrities ranging from Cindy Crawford (model and film star), Lisa Loeb (singer), Charles Shaughnessy (co-star, "The Nanny"), Reba McEntire (singer, entertainer), Richard Karn (co-star, "Home Improvement") and Spencer Christian (TV meteorologist) to former Senator John Glenn have championed the cause by taking time from their busy schedules to write letters to kids.

In 1999, Camp Fire Boys and Girls councils across the country regionalized the national call to action with unique events and promotions. In Atlanta alone, the Camp Fire Boys and Girls, Georgia Council, collaborated with companies and organizations to write 60,000 letters filled with love and appreciation to all the students in the Atlanta Public Schools. On *Absolutely Incredible Kid Day*, businesspeople, tourists and college students dropped off their letters at an event at The Mall at Peachtree Center.

AND, THERE'S MORE:

• Senior centers in Texas participated by writing, not only to young children, but to their own adult children, who were in their 30s and 40s. Some seniors wrote in their native Spanish language, and center employees translated for them.

• Athletes at Drury College and Southwest Missouri State University, Springfield, Mo., wrote letters to hospitalized children. Members from the local Camp Fire Boys and Girls council then delivered the letters and meals to children's families who were staying at the Ronald McDonald House.

• Ruth Ann Willsey, a grandmother who had been out of contact with two of her grandchildren due to a divorce, read a letter to her grandchildren over the phone and now enjoys a new relationship with both children. She also corresponds regularly with all nine of her grandchildren, telling them how absolutely incredible they are.

• A 12-year-old burn victim at Parkland Hospital, Dallas, received a letter from a local Camp Fire Boys and Girls member, encouraging him to focus on life beyond his burn injuries. Hospital staff reported marked improvement in the child's morale.

• Tana Fedric, a member of the First Texas Council of Camp Fire, Fort Worth, decided to jot down on paper some affirming thoughts about her 19-year-old son. A few months later, he died unexpectedly. She told others about writing that letter to her son in a moving letter to the editor to persuade parents and adults to participate in Camp Fire Boys and Girls' *Absolutely Incredible Kid Day*.

What we've learned is that *Absolutely Incredible Kid Day* changes lives. Kids of all cultures and ages have tucked their letters into scrapbooks, shoeboxes and billfolds. Some letters have been framed and hung on walls.

In its first three years, more than 300 million people heard about the letter-writing campaign. If each listener, each TV viewer and each magazine reader wrote just one letter, every child in America would receive a letter of love and encouragement. Imagine what that would do to encourage our nation's youth!

After three years of celebrating thousands of letters, we thought we'd share some of the most touching with you. We are deeply grateful to the moms and dads, volunteers, mentors, grandparents and celebrities who bring meaning to this wonderful day for kids. These letter writers have made *Absolutely Incredible Kid Day* a winner and have helped Camp Fire Boys and Girls put smiles on the faces of millions of kids.

Absolutely Incredible Letters to Kids:

You Deserve Applause

Dear Ms. Emily

Another year has gone by and I've had the opportunity to watch you grow - not only up, but mentally, socially and spiritually. I am very proud of the effort that you put forth in school. I absolutely love going to the awards ceremonies to watch you be acknowledged for honor roll. It's also been fun watching you gain confidence in playing soccer and basketball. When you scored your first basket I was the most elated person in the gym, except for maybe you. I'm also very pleased that you're participating in youth group at church. It is a very worthwhile way to spend your time - worshipping and sharing spiritual fellowship.

Emily, you are truly an outstanding person. I can see by your daily activities and by the friends that you choose that you have a keen sense of knowing right from wrong. To have you as a daughter makes me the luckiest person on earth.

Never ending love,
Dad

"**W**hat I wanted to say to Emily came very naturally. I don't usually write stuff like this, but I thought it would be a good idea to let my daughter know that I loved her. I get accused of being quiet and introspective. Too often, I hold my feelings in. This letter gave me a chance to tell Emily that I love her when I can't always say the words out loud. She flashed a huge smile and gave me a big thank-you hug for the letter. Someday, I'll probably write her another letter."

— Mark Matson, *Emily's dad*

Dear Tina,

Grandpa and I want to thank you for inviting us to come and watch you swim in the district meet. I'm sure that must have been a little scary, being your first time, and at a strange pool with so many people watching. But you did so great, even breaking your own qualifying time in the freestyle.

If you do your best at whatever you try, you can always be proud of yourself, and we are proud of you.

Love,

Grandma & Grandpa

ATLANTA PUBLIC SCHOOLS

OFFICE OF THE SUPERINTENDENT

Focus on Student Success

March 18, 1999

TO: Atlanta Public Schools' Incredible Kids

I have had the pleasure of serving you, the students of Atlanta Public Schools, for over thirty-six years. It has always been evident to me that you are, without a doubt, Absolutely Incredible Kids!

As students, you may not always realize the value you bring to the lives of adults. Each day we experience something different through your eyes. Sometimes those experiences may make us laugh and sometimes they may make us cry. But whatever emotion they bring, those experiences give us the ability to understand your circumstances and guide you through the challenges of life. You give us a sense of purpose and help us to understand that you are our future, our most valued resource and our greatest treasure.

Remember … the best motivation is self-motivation. Therefore, if after today those around you forget to remind you how wonderful you are, before going to bed or upon rising, look in the mirror and say to yourself, "It's true … I am an Absolutely Incredible Kid!"

Sincerely,

Betty L. Strickland, Ed.D.
Interim Superintendent

"I didn't know Marquita before I wrote this letter, but my company asked us to write letters to kids on *Absolutely Incredible Kid Day*. When I saw a list of kids with special names, I was drawn to the description of this beautiful girl. I selected Marquita because I wanted to encourage her to follow her dreams. I believe everyone can be whatever he or she chooses, regardless of background, if given the right kind of encouragement. I wanted to encourage her to stay true to herself and tell her she could accomplish anything she set her mind to do. My company threw a party for the kids and presented them with their letters. I hope to hear from Marquita someday and find out that she's fulfilling her dreams."

— Brenda Nightingale, *employee volunteer*

HOT NEWS!

Dear Marquita,

So you love to play basketball? Are you good enough, they will say? Are you smart enough, they will say? Are you focused, they will say?

I say, YES! Marquita is all that and more! All you have to do is learn the right direction to take *and* learn the game of life and the game of basketball. You can be good enough, you are smart enough and you can be focused on the goal. Whether the goal is a basketball goal or a goal for your life, you can train and discipline yourself to be a winner in the basketball arena *and* in the game of life.

It is all up to you. Learn how to use the resources available and search and find the ones that are not. Be proud, take pride, give and demand respect, have impeccable integrity, be sincere, learn to speak warmly and graciously, and be true to yourself.

I Love and Believe in You.

Brenda

"I had been focusing on myself for a long time. I moved away from my family to New York City, began a new job, and hadn't really focused on Jonathan in a while. I wanted to focus on him for a minute — to make some time for him. My brother has Down's Syndrome. He's had numerous personal challenges related to his health. Through it all, his focus was never on himself, but on my parents and me. Due to the Down's Syndrome, Jonathan has trouble reading. My mother read my letter to him, and they both started crying. He called me right away to thank me and told me, 'You always make me cry, Ronda.'"

— Ronda Music, *Jonathan's Sister*

Dear Jonathan,

I realized that in my busy life, so far from home, I rarely take the time to let you know how much you are loved, and how thoughts of you fill my day — every day. Marlin and I often tell stories about you, and discuss your achievements. We laugh at your humor and remember the scent of your hugs and the joy of your kisses. I have a picture of you and me from that little photo booth at the mall where you are hugging me with such a grin on your face — and I notice that while I look happy, I know the moment is rare, and never enough to make up for the time I am away from home.

You see, Jonathan: I don't know how to tell you the utter joy you bring to so many people. You are so brave and funny, so smart and with such a personality, I have no doubt that you will change the world as you have changed mine ...

... I read a book the other day that spoke of the challenges of life and what people consider necessary to be happy. I realized that with all the struggles in our family — with Mom and Dad living apart now and with new people in their lives — with your personal challenges — from all the heart surgeries where you were so brave and now pushing through the restrictions people may create for you because you are Down's Syndrome — you PREVAIL. When I had my surgery last year, and was so frightened — I remembered you going into one of your heart operations, holding onto your Hulk Hogan figure, and telling me, and Mom and Dad, Old One and all of US, to be brave, that you would be all right. You probably don't remember that, Jonathan; you were only 4 years old.

I hope you realize, Jon, all of your accomplishments. I hope you will know that you are the riches of the world, a star in the sky ...
I love you, Jon Orf.

Big Hug ... Big Kiss ... Rub it in

Ronda

3/18/89

Jessica,

I am writing to you on absolutely incredible kid day. And since you are one of my incredible kids, you qualify!!

I have been bragging about you here at work because of your being selected for the cheerleading team. I know it took a lot of hard work & courage to compete & practice. I will be a "proud papa" in the stands, watching you and your team next year.

I looked over your progress report last night & can see the improvement being made in algebra - keep up the studying & hard work & it will all come together in class.

Well, have a good day & I love you,

Dad

Dear Kristen,

Today is absolutely incredible kids day. You are so very special to me, I am so proud of all of your accomplishments. Keep up the great work. You have a heart as big as Texas and I love it when you sprinkle your happy dust on your friends and family and even people you do not know.

Love Mommy

:-)

Dear Anthony,

Hello! March 18th is Incredible Kids Day. And do you know what?
I think you are the most incredible, helpful, wonderful kid on the planet!!
Whoever knew a ten-year old boy could do so much to help everyone
he knows? Whoever knew a ten-year old boy could be so smart?
I don't know, but it's all in you, my cool little brother! Always helping
Kuya when he can't write out or read his homework, or helping me
separate the clothes for the laundry. Also, thanks for always getting
the cordless phone when we were all too lazy! Anthony, you were
always listening whenever I would tell a story, even though everyone
had already stopped listening!! Anthony, you are so funny when you copy
The Simpsons! And you've come to be such an awesome dancer!
You're even better than me sometimes! WOW! You are so cool!
Basically, I'm giving this to you to tell you how special you are:
to me, to your Kuya, to family. We love you.

Love,
Ate

*NOTE: "Kuya" means older brother and "Ate" (AH-teh) means
  older sister in Tagalog, the native language of the Philippines.

Absolutely Incredible Letters to Kids:

You Make Me Smile

"The biggest kid in my life is my 83-year-old grandfather. He's my friend. He's childlike, and I often try to remind him how important he is to me, even though we're miles away. That's why I sent him a letter on *Absolutely Incredible Kid Day*. Grandpa called me after he received the letter and told me he'd hung it in his bedroom at wheelchair level, and said he thinks of me every time he enters the room."

— Julie duChene, *granddaughter*

March 16, 1999

Dear Grandpa,

We received a memo at work about the Camp Fire Boys and Girls' Incredible Kid Day, where they encourage you to write letters to kids to let them know how special they are!

Well, I can't think of a bigger or more special kid than you! You've been my buddy and friend and "silly old Grandpa" for over 42 years now and I consider myself a very lucky person. I'm so thankful that my Grandma is such a smart woman and married such a caring, loving person who has been an incredible asset to our family.

I wish we lived closer so we could spend more time together. I cherish my growing up years when we did live close and were able to spend so many wonderful times together. I'll never forget how special it was to be able to spend a weekend at your house (without my siblings!) and sew with Grandma. I've never gone back to Yosemite but I will remember all the fun the 3 of us had together on that trip (and Grandma's sacrificial magazine when I got carsick!!)

There are so may good memories and happy times. I look forward to seeing you both again soon and adding some more great memories to the old ones.

Thanks for being you, Grandpa.

Love from your "kid,"

Julie

Julie

10 MARCH 1999

DEAR GISELLE --

ONCE THERE WAS JUST YOUR DADDY AND I.
OFTEN WE DREAMED OF HAVING OUR OWN
BABY.
FINALLY AFTER A LONG, LONG WHILE WE
WERE BLESSED WITH THE BIRTH OF OUR
LITTLE DAUGHTER, GISELLE.
GISELLE, YOU ARE MORE THAN WE HOPED
FOR.
YOUR EYES SPARKLE IN THE AMAZEMENT
OF CHILDHOOD CURIOSITY.
YOUR SMILE LIGHTS UP THE WORLD.
YOU GIGGLE WITH GIRLISH GLEE
YOUR BOUNDLESS ENERGY KEEPS YOUR
MUM FOREVER YOUNG.
YOUR HUGS ARE PRICELESS.
YOU ARE INCREDIBLE ... BECAUSE
        YOU ARE YOU ... BECAUSE
        WE ARE BLESSED BY YOU
        IN OUR WORLD.

    WE LOVE YOU,
    MUM AND DADDY
    (SANDRA AND CARLOS)

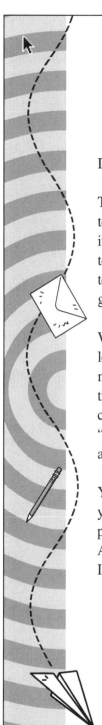

Dear Billy & Joey,

The purpose of this letter is to express how happy I am to have you both as part of my family, how much pleasure it has given me to become your grandma. It is so very nice to have two more grandchildren, two more grandsons, to even out the number of wonderful grandsons and granddaughters I now have.

When your mother started dating my son and they came to love each other, I worried that you boys might not like me, might not want me to be your grandmother. I knew the first time I met the two of you that I loved you right away and could hardly wait to start being your grandma; to be able to "baby-sit" for you as grandmas do; to be able to buy birthday and Christmas presents for you; to show my love for you.

You have no idea how wonderful it makes me feel to have you call me grandma and to tell me you love me. I am so proud to be a grandma to two such sweet and loving boys. Along with your sister you are definitely the joys of my life. I love you both so very much.

Love & kisses,

Grandma

:-)

Camp Fire
Boys and Girls®

SOUTHWEST AIRLINES
A SYMBOL OF FREEDOM™

YAHOO!™

Dear Jordan,
aka: Jo-Jo, Jo, Jo-Bear, Jordy

You are the love of my life. I just want you to know how much you
are truly loved. I enjoy every moment with you. When I wake up in
the morning and peek at you in your room, you look so cute with
your rumpled hair and peaceful look on your face. I know you
are dreaming of all the fun things the day has in store for you. I love
to eat breakfast with you each morning together before I go off to work.
I love the way you get excited about going to preschool. I am amazed
at how much you are learning. You are like a little sponge, soaking up
information about everything. I love the way you say Grace before
each meal and you are learning how wonderful God is. I love the way
you cry when others cry around you; it shows how compassionate
you are at such a young age. I love the way you sing, "Twinkle, Twinkle,
Little Star. How I wonder what you are. Up a ba ba ba ba ba so high, like
a diamond in the sky." Your daddy has a hard time remembering all the
words to songs too! I love the great big giant hugs we share. I love the
way you say "Thank You" and "Please" to everyone. Your teacher says
you are the most polite student she has ever had. You make me so
proud. I love the way we say our prayers each night and I kiss your
eyes closed so you will have sweet dreams. I love tucking you into
bed and knowing that you are "snug as a bug in a rug." I love it when
you laugh and giggle. And when we play "Where is me?" I love the
way you get excited about the little things; everything is an adventure
for you. I love the way we hold hands when we walk. I know each
moment how blessed I am to have a special child like you. At the end
of the day, I say a prayer of thanksgiving, as I know no other love
greater than what I have for you. You are my awesome opossum!
I will love you forever!!!

XOXO,

Mommy

"**J**ordan was still a toddler when I wrote this letter to her. She is such an important part of our life and I wanted to do something special to honor her, even though she was too young to comprehend it. That night as I was reading the letter to her, I was the one who got choked up, but I think she understood what I wanted to give to her. I guess it was the way I smiled at her that made her cover me with kisses. That night, she didn't fuss before going to sleep. She simply rolled over and closed her eyes. I still remember watching her as she drifted off to sleep."

— Deborah Morrison, *Jordan's mom*

Dear Daniel,

I wanted to take a moment to tell you how special and important you are and to thank you for all the things you say and do to make my life happy and full. I learn so much from you every day, and I want you to know what a privilege it is being your mother.

Thank you for reminding me that it's fun to roll down a grassy hill, to jump in puddles and to tickle someone until they laugh out loud.

I forgot that clouds make pictures in the sky, that seashells tell you where they've been, and that butterfly kisses are so soft. You help me remember.

When I see your mischievous smile and twinkle in those big blue eyes, I forget about grass stains on the knees of new pants, Kool-Aid spilled on the carpet, and finger prints on windows.

It's amazing to me still, how I cover my ears to the alarm and roll over in agony at the thought of rising in the morning, but I can bolt from deep sleep at the sound of your voice in the middle of the night.

When you cry, when there's pain in your eyes, I remember how hard it is growing up, how confusing and difficult life can seem, and I realize you have demands to meet also.

When I lose sight of you in a crowd or at the beach, I know true fear. In those seconds my eyes search for you, I'm no longer worried about everyday concerns. The workload, the bills and car troubles vanish from thought, and I long for nothing more than to hold you in my arms and hear your voice again.

Even when you wipe my kisses off and struggle free as I wipe the ice cream off your face, I smile and laugh. I know someday I won't be so needed, and I'll long for those moments again.

I watch you work so hard, accomplishing and thriving and growing, and my heart swells with love and admiration. I wonder what it is I've done to deserve such an incredible soul in my life. You make me proud and I tell everyone, "That's my son."

Since you've come into my life, I've learned to talk less and listen more, to slow down and notice the world around me, and to look for the good in everyone. I stopped looking so far into the future, and concentrate more on today.

Most importantly, Daniel, you have taught me the true meaning of love and devotion, to never lose hope, to seize every moment, and to cherish this life and all its blessings.

Thank you, son, for taking the time to teach me.

Love,
Mom

"I waited until the kids were in bed and the house was quiet, sat down at the computer and started writing. I was crying as I wrote the letter. I wanted to tell Daniel how special he was and how proud of him I was. I had Daniel when I was 17, and we've both grown up so much together. I read the letter to Daniel who intently listened. He blushed a few times, but he hugged and kissed me, thanked me, and asked me to save it for him. I plan to pull the letter out when he enters his teens as a reminder that I did, and still do, love him!"

— Stacie Perrine, *Daniel's mom*

Dear Ashley Poo!   March 18, 1999
Today is a special day. It is a day
to tell any kid how special they are.
Kind of like Mother's Day, but for
kids.
I just want to tell you how very
special you are to me. Every day
you make me smile a hundred
times.
I hope you never stop giving me a
million hugs and kisses a week.
Your laughter and cutesy words, such
as naynaise (mayonaise) lickstip (lipstick)
and oat-me-meal, brighten my
heart ♡. You are the greatest kid
in the world. I love you Pumba!
                    Love Momma

3-19-98

Dear Lindsey,

This is your day to hear what you should hear every day. You are a marvellous child! Every day I still feel lucky to be your daddy. Your talents, abilities, and personality are all gifts. They help make you the wonderful girl that you are.

You're growing up just right, so please keep it up. I hope that you'll always feel how special you really are, and never lose confidence in how much I really do love you

Love,
Daddy

"It seemed that Kelly and I hardly saw each other anymore. Even though we lived in the same house, we were both working, and our personal activities kept us from doing what we used to do as a mother and daughter. In previous years, I'd been a Camp Fire leader, so when I heard about *Absolutely Incredible Kid Day*, I thought it might be nice to surprise my daughter with a little motherly warmth. It had been a long time since I'd seen tears in my daughter's eyes. I don't think I'll wait so long before I write a letter to her again."

— Derry Winch, *Kelly's mom*

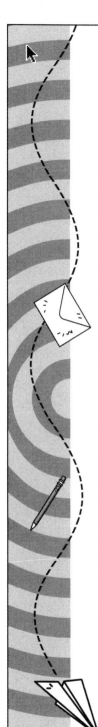

Dear Kelly,

Know what I like about you? It's those little things that you do that mean so much to me. Like remembering to fill the humidifier with water when I get too busy to notice that the refill light is on! Or, when you came home and bought me a couple of pairs of socks, just because you heard me say, "I need socks."

You are an incredible kid for doing things like the time I was sick in bed with the flu. I will never forget you coming in my room with a paper nurse's cap on, pad of paper and pen in hand, to take my "order" for juice, or whatever I wanted to eat (not that I COULD eat), but that made me feel SO much better.

You are an incredible kid because you know how I feel and you know what I am thinking. I love the way we can hear or see something, look at each other, be thinking the same thing, and, without saying a word we both laugh!

I love you, you incredible kid!

E-mail

SUBJECT: Absolutely Incredible Kid Day
FROM: Patty Rice
DATE: 3/18/99

Dear Katherine,

Do you know what I like about you?

I like your beautiful soul.
I like the way you treat others.
I like that you're a sensitive person.
I like how you love animals.
I like how you care about people.
I like that you respect yourself.
I like your funny sense of humor.
I like your open-mindedness.
I like that you can be open-minded without
losing sight of who you are.
I like that you can laugh at yourself.
I like your good nature and big heart.
I like that you write notes to your friends every day.
I like how you "IM" three friends all at once
when you're on-line.
I like your smile.
I love you.

Mom

"I was in the middle of a huge project at work when our employer encouraged us to write a letter to a child on *Absolutely Incredible Kid Day*. My teenage daughter, Katherine, is such a good friend to her friends, and I wanted her to know that I value her compassion for others. I e-mailed a note to Katherine, but she received it before I could get home and watch her expression. She never really said anything to me, but I noticed she'd taped the note to her vanity mirror next to pictures of her friends and important keepsakes. That was all the affirmation I needed to know I had done the right thing. I hope all parents get the feeling I did when I saw that note on her mirror."

— Patty Rice, *Katherine's mom*

Dear Bethany,

I am writing you this letter in celebration of INCREDIBLE KID DAY. I don't always say enough "I love you"s so I'm glad you remind me to every day, "forever and ever."

You are only five but want so much to be as big as Dane. Although I'm resisting it I know I have to let you grow up. I love how you rub it in with your "Ha! Ha! I'm big now," whenever you discover you can do something on your own. You make me think about the little things I take for granted, like pouring your own juice, opening the car door or putting on your own shoes. You really believe "just three more inches" will make you a giant.

I love watching you grow out of your clothes and picking out new ones with you, reading with you and all your fifty million questions.

I just want you to remember that you are a great kid, smart and funny, making me laugh more than I thought I could. You and Daney gave me a chance to grow up all over again and I'm having so much fun!

Love,
Mommy

16 March 1999

Hi Ashley,

This is a surprise letter. It isn't your birthday. It isn't Christmas. You've already lost all of your baby teeth (we think 😊). It's just an out of the blue letter to let you know that we think you're an absolutely InCrEdIbLe Kid.

When we see you with little Delaney or with Zsuzsa, Michael and Marcus, you always set a good example for the younger kids. We're sure you're a good role model for Donovan and Jared too. We notice how you are always patient when it comes to opening presents at Christmas, handing the gifts to the little ones who get so excited they can't wait. We also notice how good you are at memorizing the poems you learn at school and how much you like to read - just like we do.

And... you're a fellow Spice Girls fan, which is definitely a plus. Someday we'll have to watch the video together. Anyway, we just thought that we'd tell you that whether you're with your mom in Elk Grove or your dad in Pleasanton, at school or just relaxing around the house, singing or dancing, we think you're one cool kid!

Just tellin' you what we think, what we really really think (sing that to the tune of "So tell me what you want, what you really, really want") - Uncle Louis and Aunt Lisa

"For six years now, I have written notes to my daughter, Pancha, and quietly tucked them into her lunch box. She always pretends to be surprised to find them, but I know that she looks forward to reading a little note from home when she opens her lunch. Call it a security blanket, or just a bit of serendipity in an otherwise structured school day. Once, when I was in a mad dash to get Pancha off to school and myself off to work, I forgot to include that little bit of homemade love in her lunch box. She let me know as soon as I picked her up from school that it made her sad not to have the midday connection with home that she had come to expect.

We adopted Pancha from an orphanage in South America when she was a toddler. It was love at first sight for her dad and me. One look at those sparkling dark eyes and the contagious grin on her little face, and we knew that God had given us the gift of a lifetime. Even though I have always worked, my priorities shifted as soon as I became a mom. Drawing picture notes to my preschool daughter (I♥U) became more important to me than the reports I wrote at work. As the years passed, the little scribbled picture notes turned into jokes, limericks and brief letters from the dog. She often shares the silliest ones with her friends, and sometimes with her teachers.

Not long ago, I opened a sandwich wrapper in the "working lunch" I had stuck in my briefcase, and found a small piece of paper that read, "Mom, I love you so much. I hope you have a great day. Love, Pancha." Those few words on paper, which express what all parents hold in their hearts for their children, were coming back to me from a third grader who has already learned some of life's most important lessons."

— Ann Powell-Brown, *Pancha's mother*

Dear Pancha,
We love your head,
We love your toes.
And in your book
Please keep your nose
So you can learn
Before you play.
Enjoy your friends!
Enjoy your day!
Love, Mom & Dad

Dear Pancha,
I guess I have to stay
home with the cat.
You know that I'm not
happy with that.
But study hard, and
have some fun,
And we'll run and play
when school is done.

Love, Your dog Zoe

Dear Pancha,
I saw your lunch.
You packed a bunch!
Don't mean to be rude.
You need that food
So you don't have to strain
When you use your good brain!
Love, Mom

I once knew a girl
quite small,
Who was fast on her feet
with a ball,
Nobody could knock her
When she played soccer
She played like one
seven feet tall!
Happy soccer practice today!
Love, Mom

Absolutely Incredible
Letters to Kids:

You Give Me Hope
When Times are Tough

"I'd love for my son, Christopher, and my daughter, Katie, to someday look back at their scrapbooks and feel a sense of warmth about special times in their lives. So, when I saw the banner on the Internet promoting *Absolutely Incredible Kid Day*, I thought this would be a wonderful way to add a message to their books. I wanted each of them to have a positive sense of who they were, and I also wanted to immediately reward them for their recent great behavior. After writing a letter to both of them, I waited awhile before giving it to my son. Christopher, a busy 6-year-old, watched me with these huge curious eyes as I read the letter to him. He gave me a big hug and a kiss. I think he was as proud of the message as he was that his mommy had written a letter to him."

— Susie Orlady, *Christopher and Katie's mom*

MARCH 17, 1999

MY DEAREST CHRISTOPHER:

YOU ARE AN ABSOLUTELY
INCREDIBLE KID! THE PAST YEAR
HAS BEEN VERY HARD ON YOU
SINCE GRAMMY VERA WAS SICK
WITH CANCER — YOU HAVE
BRIGHTENED UP SO MANY OF
MY BLUE DAYS WITH YOUR
DEAR SWEET COMMENTS . . . .
"MOMMY, DON'T BE SAD, YOU CAN
WRITE GRAMMY A LETTER . . . YOU CAN
VISIT HER IN A DREAM . . . I
KNOW HOW HARD IT IS FOR YOU
SINCE GRAMMY VERA DIED, BUT SHE
IS WITH GRANDPA WARREN."
THANK YOU LITTLE BEAR FOR YOUR
SILLY JOKES THAT YOU HOPED WOULD
CHEER ME UP AND BRING A SMILE
TO MY FACE. I LOVE THE SUPRISE
HUES AND GLANCES YOU GIVE ME
AS YOUR EYEBROWS RAISE AND
YOU SMILE AT ME —
YOU ARE MY BUDDY BEAR —
          LOVE,
              MOMMY

MARCH 17, 1999

MY DEAREST KATIE:
WHAT AN INCREDIBLE KID YOU ARE!
YOU ARE WISE BEYOND YOUR
YEARS — ONE DAY SHORTLY AFTER
MY MOTHER'S DEATH, I WAS IN
TEARS — AS I TURNED TO YOU
AND SAID, " OH, KATIE WHAT AM I
GOING TO DO? I MISS GRAMMY
SO MUCH." YOU SAID ... " ONE DAY
AT A TIME MOMMY, ONE DAY AT
A TIME ..." HOW CAN A 2½ YEAR
OLD HAVE SUCH WISDOM?
YOU ALWAYS BRING A SMILE TO MY
FACE AS YOU SPORT YOUR ZAINY GET-
UPS AND CART AROUND YOUR
COLLECTION OF TRAVEL SOAPS, YOUR
SPATULA AND MINI TUBES OF
TOOTHPASTE. — ONCE AGAIN LAST
WEEK AS I WAS HAVING A DOWN
DAY, HIDING MY FACE IN TEARS
YOU SAID, "MOMMY, DON'T CRY I
CAN'T SEE YOUR PRETTY EYES WHEN
YOU HIDE THEM." "REMEMBER, GRAMMY
WILL ALWAYS BE IN YOUR HEART."
KATIE, THE ANGELS BLESSED ME
THE DAY YOU WERE BORN —
I LOVE YOU SO!
LOVE,
MOMMY

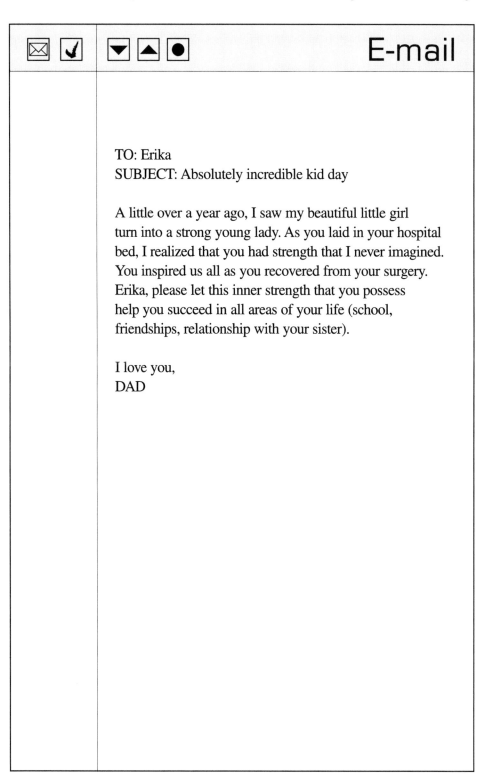

TO: Erika
SUBJECT: Absolutely incredible kid day

A little over a year ago, I saw my beautiful little girl
turn into a strong young lady. As you laid in your hospital
bed, I realized that you had strength that I never imagined.
You inspired us all as you recovered from your surgery.
Erika, please let this inner strength that you possess
help you succeed in all areas of your life (school,
friendships, relationship with your sister).

I love you,
DAD

March 16, 1999

Dear Roscoe:

I am writing you this letter to tell you what an Absolutely Incredible kid you are! You are a happy, outgoing kid with a smile that lights up any room. I know that things have been tough for you right now. Middle school is difficult, and your grades are not as good as they used to be. However, I believe in you, and I know you will turn this around. Just hold on and keep pressing forward. Things will get better. Just know that I am always here for you to listen to you, laugh with you, and to cry with you. Even to guide you as you face these sometimes difficult years. But I know you can do it. I believe in you. *REMEMBER YOU'RE A WINNER!*

Roscoe, I love you very much. You have always been a joy to me. I look at your pictures and in every single one you have a big wonderful smile, except when you're sleeping, of course. Don't give up, don't quit. This too will pass. I am in your corner and walking with you down this tunnel of difficulty. Keep looking forward. This light is straight ahead. That light is the light of victory, overcoming, and better grades.

Love always,

Mom

Camp Fire
Boys and Girls®

SOUTHWEST AIRLINES
A SYMBOL OF FREEDOM™

YAHOO!™

Dear April,

March 18 is **Absolutely Incredible Kid Day** and since you are an **Absolutely Incredible Kid**, Grandpa and I want you to know how much we love you and how proud we are of you for all your wonderful accomplishments. Like getting good grades in School and doing your very best in all the sports you are involved in.

You have had to grow up years before you should have. How you were able to compose and read the wonderful tribute you wrote about your parents, at your Dad's funeral? Also, how you have accepted the responsibility of helping Mom at home and taking wonderful care of your brother Tyler.

Your energy, enthusiasm and new ideas will help to make our world a better place. You have great value, and you deserve to be heard.

     Reach for the sky!!
     Follow your dreams!! (Like going to K-State)
     Love yourself!!

Love Always,

Grandma Shirley
Grandpa Bill

Grandma Shirley and Grandpa Bill

47

Absolutely Incredible Letters to Kids:

I Love Watching You Grow

March 18, 1999

Dear Shane,

I'm writing to you on Absolutely Incredible Kid Day to let you know that I love you, and that I think you are an incredible kid and an incredible person. You make me incredibly happy! Sometimes I forget to tell you, so I'm writing you this letter so you will know.

I love you. I'm honored to be your mom and consider it, along with being married to your dad, as the greatest, most wonderful thing in my life. I feel so much pride whenever I think of you!

There is nothing that you could ever do that would stop me from loving you. No matter how you look or whether you get good grades or not — I'll always be proud of you, and will always love you!

I wish I could make it so you are always happy and content and healthy and strong.

I'm very glad you had fun during your spring break and am glad you made it back safe and sound. I miss you and hope you'll come home soon for a visit!

Love always,
Mom

Dear Justin,

I'm sitting at my computer at the office and thought I would write
you a letter and say "hello" and tell you that I think you are wonderful!

I'm sorry I don't see you more often than I do. I hope maybe at Easter
time there will be another family gathering and you will be there.
Oh, I know, I bet you might be at the birthday party for Gagie
on March 10 (Sunday).

Anyway, I think that you are a very talented person. I really enjoyed
seeing you in the play about Akito. Did I spell the character's name
right? I think you are very good at singing and at remembering
your lines.

Also, you are just extremely nice to be around. I remember how nice
you were to your cousin Wesley the time she was here for Thanksgiving.
She was feeling pretty shy, but you really made her feel at home.
You were so smiley and friendly and you showed her all your toys.
And you always give me a big hug and a kiss whenever I come to
your house, which makes me feel great.

I hope everything is going really well at school and that there will
soon be some nice warm weather so you can play outdoors. I wonder
if you will be playing Little League baseball this spring. Maybe
I could come watch a game.

Lots of love to a pretty incredible kid,

Aunt Anne

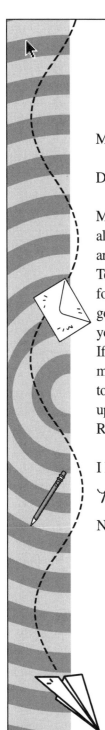

March 18, 1999

Dear Gregory,

My Bubba! You are so full of life and excitement! You are always ready to play and have fun. I love to watch you run around the house so full of energy. You are a great basketball, Tee-ball and soccer player. Someday I bet you'll be into football too! You are great in math, reading, and you do really good with your spelling words too. I love for you to tell me your jokes! Thank you so much for your *hugs and kisses*! If I had kids, I would want one just like you! You always make me smile, even when you're in trouble! I'm very lucky to get to share in your life everyday and watch you grow up to be a wonderful young man. I love you very much! Remember to study hard, play hard and have a wonderful life.

I love you,

No-No

No-No (Aunt Nora)

:-)

Camp Fire
Boys and Girls®

SOUTHWEST AIRLINES
A SYMBOL OF FREEDOM™

YAHOO!

"Just days before *Absolutely Incredible Kid Day*, Luke's appendix ruptured and he was rushed to the hospital for an emergency appendectomy. Luke is one of the boys who comes to my home every day for child care, and I missed having him with me during his recovery. I visited him every day while he was in the hospital. Through the recovery, and then again later when there were complications, he didn't whine or complain at all, even though he was feverish and in pain. Knowing he could have died really made me want to write him and tell him why he was special. I'm so glad I wrote to him. He and I are growing so much closer now."

— Miriam Ann Ippel, *Luke's child care provider*

March 18, 1999

Dear Luke,

Even though I get to see you often and tell you how cool I think you are, I am writing you this letter so that it will forever be written down. You are one incredible kid ☺!

I can still remember the first time I met your family when you moved on to Griswold. Joel wasn't even born yet so we got to play together just us. It's amazing to me that now you're 8½ and in third grade. I am so proud of you with all your reading. You also amaze me with all your Iditarod knowledge. I hope you always have something to be excited about in school. You are also a wonderful big brother to Joel and Mark. I love playing with all of you and watching you work together and make sure everyone is safe. You are also incredibly brave. What a trooper you were in the hospital in December! If I ever have to be in the hospital I hope I do as well as you did!

Luke Andrew DeJong, you are an absolutely incredible kid and I love you very much!

&/Miriam Ann Ippel

To my *Absolutely Incredible Kids* —
Danielle, Kimberlee & Kiersten,

I am writing to let you know just how ***absolutely incredible***
you are! All three of you are special, unique and ultimately
priceless. No one in the world is just like you. Every day,
you make me proud to be your mom. I love you kids
more than anything in this world.

I encourage you to dream your dream every day. Do as
well as you can in everything you do. The sports, dancing,
hobbies and homework you do today will bring you
happiness and success later in life. I want you to have
lots of fun in the process! Live your life as you would
climb a mountain. Climb slowly, steadily, and enjoy
each passing moment.

Remember — you can achieve anything and everything
you want to. I believe in you! Reach for the sky!

I love you kids very, very much!

Mom

:-)

Dear Gabrielle:

Even at 4 years of age, I marvel at your enthusiasm, and how each day you wake up everyone with your radiant smile and expressive hands as you tell them "Its Morning". The pure joy you experience playing Outside, seeing, touching, running, playing on your toys. Everything is fun for you. I'm Amazed at your seriousness taking ballet lessons, Always smiling. The beginning of your Artistic abilities developing. All of these, and Much More qualifies you as an "Absolutely Incredible Kid!"

Your friendliness & your ability to Make Conversation With Anyone is a gift. You Are experiencing life at its fullness

You Are special.

Sincerely
Dot Osborn

Dear Victoria,

You are absolutely an incredible kid. From the day you were born a unique bond was created between us. I look at you and feel love, happiness, and excitement. These feelings grow with each passing day.

There are so many things I love about you. One of my favorite things is how you always manage to make me smile. You make me giggle when you do silly things such as hide under a blanket to peek at me, put a bowl on your head as a hat, or dance with me around the living room.

I often call you my little parrot. It makes me feel special when you copy what I say or do. My heart fills with joy when you come down the hall wearing my shoes, push a chair over to the sink to help me wash dishes, or have to wear the same color shirt I am wearing.

I find your love of learning exciting. It is a wonderful feeling seeing things for the first time through your eyes. You make situations together facinating and fun. I like going on our family day trips to the zoo, aquarium, and Sesame Street Live.

But I also love the little things we do together. How you like to sing songs in the car, name the colors of the crayons as we draw, and count the stairs as we slide down them.

Victoria, you are truly the sunshine of my life. Just thinking of you brings to me the biggest smile and warmest feelings. You are in every way possible an incredible kid.

Love,
Mommy
xoxo

"The staff at my daughter's family day care center told me about *Absolutely Incredible Kid Day* when I dropped Victoria off that morning. All day long, I thought about things I'd like to say to her in a letter. At the end of the day, I was so tired from work, but that night, I decided to give her a written snapshot of her life when she was 2 years old. My husband and I had waited such a long time to have a child, so the letter was as much for both of us as it was for Victoria. I'm saving her letter in a scrapbook, next to letters Victoria also received from her father and grandmother on *Absolutely Incredible Kid Day*."

— Michelle Walsh, *Victoria's mom*

Dear Ilana,

To my little sister who is now a teenager. I am so proud of the person
you are. You have always been your own person, no matter what
the pressures that you were receiving from two domineering older
siblings. Every time we told you how to think or what to do, you'd put
those little fists on your hips and stare us down — even as a two-year-old.

I know that we have had our sibling problems, but I will always love
you so much. You are an amazing person. I guess your brother and
I must have done something right. Just return that pair of shoes that
you borrowed last week.

Love,
Shoshi

To My Pooh Butt Hannah,

You were my first grandbaby, so I have a very special place in my heart for you. In my whole life, before you were born, I never knew of this different love I have for you, ofcourse no one can resist loving you, you are such a sweet, charming, and loving child. I love it when you sing & dance with me. I love to see your eyes lite up when music is played. You have your mama Di's love for music. I enjoy going places with you because we have a lot in common. I am very proud of all the things you have accomplished in a very short time, like softball, cheerleading, & gymnastics. You are very good at whatever you do. I know you will grow up and become a very special, and georgeous lady. I will always be there for you, to help in anyway I can. I love you so dearly, never forget that you have a special place in my heart. I will always remeber how we went on our first vacation together and we sang Zippady Dodah together.

I Love You,
mama Di

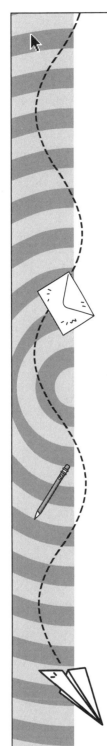

March 14, 1999

Dear Kieran,
Ever since you and your Mom moved to Louisiana, I
have been missing you more and more every day.
Even before you were born, I knew you were special.
I'm glad I was there to welcome you into the world.
You are my sweet little mister wonderful. That's why
I sing that song to you. Sweet little mister wonderful,
he's so wonderful and good, yes he is!

Do your very best at school and love your mommy.
Give her a hug each day. Do you remember the kissing
hand? That is the hand you put against your cheek
and know I would kiss you if I could and that I love
you very much!

My love to you,
Grammy

:-)

Camp Fire
Boys and Girls®

SOUTHWEST AIRLINES
A SYMBOL OF FREEDOM™

YAHOO!™

March 18, 1999

Dear Joseph,

Today is the third annual Absolutely Incredible Kid Day and I feel so lucky to have YOU as my most absolutely incredible kid!!!

I love watching you grow up (but please, slow down a little) and I love your many strengths. But I also love and understand your weaknesses too, because I see so much of myself in you. I want you to love yourself completely Joseph, not just on your good days, but ESPECIALLY on your bad ones! You need this self-love in order to become all God has intended for you, and you also need it to truly love others.

So, yes, it's true that you are terribly gifted with so many talents and wonderful strengths! You are a model son, and Dad and I are both so very proud of you. What we especially love to see in you is your perfect sense of right and wrong, and how many, many times we've been in the position to watch you do the right thing.

I know these upcoming years will be tough ones. Your teenage years I both anticipate and dread. I can't wait to see how great you turn out and at the same time, I know the mother in me will try to keep you a child for just as long as I breathe. So through this year, please keep a couple things in mind: First and foremost, I love you unconditionally. Second, you have always lived up to your name, which means "gift from God," and third — Remember, I can still beat you at chess!

Love,
Mom

"As a teacher, I know how positive notes can impact children. I read an article about *Absolutely Incredible Kid Day* in our local newspaper and felt a wave of guilt about my oldest son, Austin. I realized that after the birth of our third child, I might have been putting too much pressure on Austin to be a grown-up at a time when he still wanted to be a child. I wanted him to know why he was important to me and what made him special. The letter also allowed me to remind myself how much he really means to me. He got a big grin on his face as I read the letter to him. The next time he scored a goal, he said, "That one was for you, Mommy."

— Toni Siedel, *Austin's mom*

Austin,

Do you realize that you are one of the best parts of my day?
Well, you are. I know this because even if I'm having a bad day, if
I think about you, it makes me smile. I know this because in practically
every conversation I have, I tell a story about something you've done.
I know this because before you, I didn't realize what unconditional
love was. Here are more reasons I think you are an
"Absolutely Incredible Kid"...

• Because you tell the best silly jokes that don't always make sense,
  but always make me laugh.

• Because of the way your smile is contagious. You single-handedly
  can light up a room.

• Because you eat the pickles off of my hamburgers so I don't have to.

• Because you are a great big brother. I appreciate how you watch
  out for Taylor and Carter. No wonder they love you so much!

• Because when you make a goal in soccer, you tell me it was for me.

• Because you are a thoughtful and caring friend. Your teacher,
  Mrs. Bolte, tells me how nice to others you are.

• And because, even though I know it embarrasses you, you'll still let
  me hug you in front of your friends.

I love you, my little man!

Your mom

My Dear Julia,

I just wanted to drop you a note to let you know what an absolutely incredible kid you are. There are many reasons, but lately you have been extremely incredible and I'll tell you why ...

Thank you for always being so good to Mommy when the two of you are at home together. You know as her belly gets bigger and bigger, things she does get harder and harder. And though you are only 5 years old, you are such a big girl.

I really appreciate how you quietly keep yourself busy in the living room or in your bedroom if Mommy gets too tired and lies down for a nap. This may happen a lot more as we get closer and closer to meeting the baby brother who is growing in Mommy's belly. You're so incredible, how you watch television or work on the computer or play in your bedroom without interrupting Mommy's sleep. And I also understand that if you want a snack or something to drink, you help yourself in the kitchen without waking up Mommy.

I am very excited about the baby, Julia, and I know you are, too. Mommy tells me how you kiss and talk to her belly every day. That is great, Julia. Your brother hears you and when he comes out to meet you, he'll know just who you are!! Big Sister Julia.

You also make me very proud, how you help Mommy when the two of you go to the grocery store or have to do the laundry. You are an incredible help for both of us.

Every day, Mommy and I become more and more proud of the beautiful girl you are becoming. We both love you very much. Keep up the great work!

Love you,
Daddy

WOODROW W. (WOODY) GOSSOM, JR.

COMMISSIONER, PRECINCT NO. 1

Dear Zachary:

You are probably wondering why you are getting this letter, but that wonderment and free spirit makes you an "absolutely incredible kid." This letter is part of a National Camp Fire program, but more so, it is because you are special.

Your mother's joking about my influence on your "political" personality makes me proud, as imitation is the greatest part of flattery. However, you are your own unique, spontaneous self. I admire your open approach and enthusiasm when you undertake something.

Your efforts in Scouts and with the cello are significant. You can be whatever you desire.

Love,

Woody

*D*ana Beth Harvey, a Camp Fire Boys and Girls leader in Irving, Texas, wrote a personal letter to each club member. In each letter, she concentrated on one or more special gifts of each young person. Dana Beth Harvey represents the kind of leader we'd all like to follow. We couldn't publish each letter, but here is an excerpt from several that made us smile.

TO LOGAN:

... In addition to being intelligent and inquisitive, I've always been impressed by how caring and giving you are. No matter what we're working on, you always seem to be able to think one step ahead and come up with a suggestion for more ways we can help someone, or a better way to do something.

Even if it seems like no one in the group is listening or cares about what we're doing, I know that I can count on you to not only be focused in on what's going on, but to already be thinking of how we can do more! When you put those abilities together with your maturity and dependability, it's easy to see why I feel so lucky to have you in the club and my life.

TO STEPHANIE:

... Do you realize that we've known each other since you were in kindergarten? ... It's been such a pleasure watching you grow and mature from a cute little girl into the vibrant and beautiful young lady you have become. And I am SO proud of your many accomplishments — being chosen to sing in the Irving Girls Choir in elementary school and now in the Advanced Choir at Travis, being active at your church, playing in the band, making cheerleader two years in a row, having your emblem chosen for Camp Fire's Century Club, being a top candy seller for the past several years and now being THE top candy seller — and that's just to name a few!

TO ALEX:

It may seem that we don't know each other very well yet, but actually I've watched you from afar for many years through our various multi-group Camp Fire Boys and Girls activities. The first thing I noticed about you is how creative, outgoing and energetic you are. I can't even think of a time when I've seen you that you weren't smiling or laughing.

I know that sometimes the stuff we leaders plan doesn't always appeal to everyone in the group, but you always seem to have fun no matter where you are or what you're doing. I really admire that. I don't know if you realize it or not, but your enthusiasm and sense of fun are contagious and can bring the whole room to life.

TO KRISTEN:

Do you know that I consider you to be one of the most dependable people I know? No matter what needs to be done, you're always willing to pitch in and help, and I know I can count on you to do what you've volunteered for. That means a lot to me.

One of my favorite things about you is how happy and easy-going you are. You bring such a sense of fun to everything you do, and I love seeing you smile and hearing you laugh. Sometimes they're contagious and I can't help but to smile and laugh, too!

TO ARIANNE:

I especially want to thank you for helping me to see my son Charles in a new light. As adults, we sometimes get so caught up in being parents to our children that we overlook certain things. When I look at Charles through your eyes, I see things about him that I can't seem to focus on with my adult "parent" eyes. I appreciate you having helped me to appreciate him more.

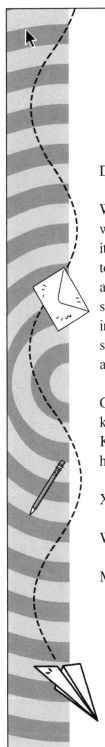

Dear Chalon (Lolo),

Whenever we think about you, our day is brighter, and
we look forward to evenings and weekends which make
it possible to spend time reading, talking, and listening
to you play the piano. You are such a sweet young lady,
and we are amazed at how fast you have grown. We can
still see you with that binki attached to your mouth, sitting
in our pool in Tucson. But we also see you in just a few
short years as a teenager on the cheerleading squad or
at a karate tournament, receiving your black belt.

Continue to work hard, and make good decisions, always
knowing how much you are loved and appreciated.
Keep up the good work in school, and don't ever forget
how proud of you we are!

XOXOXO

We love you so much!!!!

Mom & Dad

Letters to Kids From Senators, Celebrities and Sports Heroes

Reach for the sky! Follow your dreams! Love yourself!

love ya

Reba McEntire

REBA McENTIRE
Country music entertainer and film and TV performer

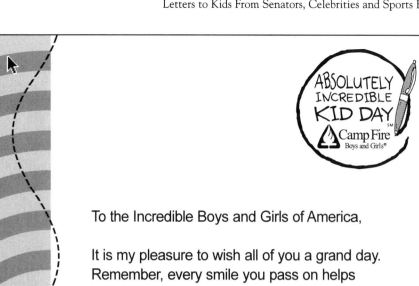

To the Incredible Boys and Girls of America,

It is my pleasure to wish all of you a grand day.
Remember, every smile you pass on helps
brighten another person's day. So, be true
to yourself, be loving and accepting of all,
and success will find you.

You are all absolutely incredible kids,
and you inspire me!

Best wishes,

Richard Karn
"Al Borland" Home Improvement

RICHARD KARN
Professional actor, Al Borland on "Home Improvement"

Susan and Charles Shaughnessy

Dear Kids,
   When you really think
about it, we're all Absolutely Incredible
Kids!... it's just that some of us have
been kids longer, so we call us Adults.
Just being who you are, the miracle
of Life that you are, makes you
Absolutely Incredible. And that won't
change for as long as you live.
Whether you become, in time, the kind
of Incredible Kid that cures cancer, wins
the Gold, holds down two jobs to
support a family, or walks on
the moon, or keeps an office building
safe and secure; remember; just
because you might look a bit
different now, you are still that
same Absolutely Incredible kid
Have a great
Life!

Charles Shaughnessy

CHARLES SHAUGHNESSY
Professional actor, Maxwell Sheffield on "The Nanny"

A letter from Charlie Schlatter

My Dearest Julia,

Eighteen months ago, an absolutely incredible prayer was answered. You were delivered to us from heaven. And from that blessed day forth, Mommy and Daddy's life together has become more and more meaningful. Your mere existence shows us the absolutely incredible capacity for love, peace and beauty this life on earth has to offer. With you in this world, all things seem possible and all things seem to make sense. As your father, I can only hope that you, too, experience the absolutely incredible feeling of joy you have enabled me to feel.

With all my deepest love,

Daddy

CHARLIE SCHLATTER
Professional actor, Dr. Jesse Travis on "Diagnosis Murder"

March 9, 1999

While I don't have any children of my own, I am lucky to have many younger fans at my shows — many of whom I get the chance to meet. Therefore, I've chosen to write a sort of "open letter" to ALL children ...

Dear Special Person:

First off, I want to congratulate you on being such a good person. How do I know that you're a good person (without having even met you)? Well — the mere fact that you're reading this tells me that you are the kind of person who (either through the Camp Fire organization or others) is not only making an effort to make themselves as good as possible ... but is also actively trying to make this world a better place.

That's the name of the game, you know ... making the world a better place. I believe strongly that we are all put on this earth to help one another. Whether it is offering to help an elderly person to cross the street safely, helping your little brother or sister with their homework, or simply going up and introducing yourself to the new kid on the first day of school — there is nothing greater than being able to have a positive influence on someone else's life.

As you grow older, you will find more and more ways to accomplish this. You could be a doctor who finds a cure for a disease, you could be a teacher who helps kids to learn about their world or you might even travel around with a guitar and make people feel better through your music. What you choose to do is not the point — the important part is that you try to do something that makes the world a better place.

Do you know what will happen if you, me, or anyone who tries to make the world a better place? ... The world will BE a better place.

From,

Lisa Loeb

LISA LOEB
Musician, professional singer and performer

CRAWDADDY PRODUCTIONS INC.

Dear Kids—
   What can I tell you that you don't already know. Anything is possible --you already know that. I guess I would only say to believe in yourself and trust your instincts. Only you know what's right for you - don't forget that. Being true to your best self is the surest way to being an incredible person.

Best of luck!

love

Cindy Crawford

P.S Being punctual never hurt anybody!

CINDY CRAWFORD
Super model and film star

March 10, 1999

Dear Kids of America,

I would like to salute you on this special day and encourage you to do your best to become absolutely incredible kids. And, you know it's a lot easier to be "incredible" than you might think. You don't have to be the best in the world at everything you do, but just making a special effort to do a really good job at whatever you do will qualify you to be called "incredible."

On this day when we recognize all of our absolutely incredible kids, I think it would be a great idea for each of you to think about things like courtesy, kindness, respect for others' feelings, and lending a helping hand. This would be a terrific example to set for anyone who wants to be an absolutely incredible kid.

Have a sunny day!

Sincerely yours,

Spencer Christian

SPENCER CHRISTIAN
TV weather reporter, San Francisco

To: My Three boys
T, Preston & Jordan

I'm writing this letter to you on Absolutely incredible Kid day to let you all know how special I think each of you are. I know you get tired of hearing my many speeches on a wide variety of issues that we seem to face everyday. I Just want you to know that they all come from the love I have for each of you.

Love Dad
Don Mattingly

P.s It Doesn't matter what happens on Life's road I will Always Love you.
DaD.

DON MATTINGLY
Former first baseman, New York Yankees

SYRACUSE
Basketball

HEAD COACH ◆ JIM BOEHEIM

An Open Letter To The Community
From Syracuse Men's Basketball Coach Jim Boeheim

Dear Adults:

As adults, we sometimes get so caught up in our own day-to-day lives that we overlook doing the little things that can have a tremendous impact on the life of a child. Kids of all ages look to the adults around them for support and to reinforce a positive self-image. More than anything else, kids need to know that they are each important and special in some way.

On Thursday, March 18th, I'd like to appeal to adults throughout Central New York to join me in reaching out to the youth in this area by taking part in *Absolutely Incredible Kid Day*. This national event, sponsored by Camp Fire Boys and Girls, encourages all adults to write a brief, but meaningful, letter to a child in their lives.

The letter doesn't have to be long, or complicated. A simple note left on the child's pillow, or tucked into a lunch box, is enough to let a child know that you think they are special.

Please help me in offering some encouragement to kids in our area. On March 18th, take a few minutes to write a letter to your child, a niece, nephew, grandchild, neighbor, or any child you know. Tell them how absolutely incredible they are to you. They'll never forget you for it!

Thank you.

Jim Boeheim
Syracuse University
Men's Basketball Coach

NCAA Final Four 1975, 1987, 1996 ◆ 20 Post Season Tournaments in 21 years ◆ Big East Tournament Champion 1981, 1988, 1992
Big East Regular Season Champion 1980, 1986, 1987, 1990, 1991

JIM BOEHEIM
Head Coach, Men's Basketball, Syracuse University, Syracuse, N.Y.

KANSAS CITY CHIEFS FOOTBALL CLUB

March 18, 1999

To: All of the Absolutely Incredible Kids of America

What a privilege it is to be able to write you this letter. I'm often asked what is the best part of my job as a professional mascot. Although there are many things I love about my job, the best part is hanging out with the kids. You see, every day I do birthday parties, school assemblies and other events where I get to be around kids, and I love it. Kids are full of excitement. Kids are incredible.

If there were one thing I could tell every kid I meet, it would be to always remember how truly special you are. God loves you and has made you a very special person. No one in all the world is just like you. You are unique.

As you go through life, remember that being rich, athletic, beautiful or famous is not what makes a person special. You always have been, and always will be, special, just because you're you. Have fun being a kid and always stay a kid at heart.

In closing, I just want to thank you all for being incredible kids and for helping to make my job so much fun.

Your Friend,

K.C. Wolf   *KC Wolf*

Charter Member of the American Football Conference of the National Football League

One Arrowhead Drive   Kansas City Missouri 64129
www.kcchiefs.com

K.C. WOLF
Mascot, Kansas City Chiefs

THE UNIVERSITY OF KANSAS
MEN'S BASKETBALL OFFICE

Roy Williams—Head Coach   **Assistants: Matt Doherty • Joe Holladay • Neil Dougherty**

To the Absolutely Incredible Kids of America:

My name is Roy Williams and I am the Head Men's Basketball Coach at the Universi⁺ of Kansas. I am so, so lucky because I am associated with so many   nderful young people here at the University of Kansas and they all stai ed out as absolutely incredible kids.

I want to encourage all of you to do a couple of things to continue being absolutely incredible kids. My first encouraging words would be for you to work extremely hard academically. Someone can take away a lot of things from you in life, but they can never take away your mind. Work very hard in the academic area so you will be able to make your own decisions and not have someone else make all of your decisions for you.

Secondly, I would ask all of you to find something that you truly love and dream about, and work as hard as you possibly can to reach those dreams. You should always aim for the stars, because you never can tell … you might hit them. I would like for you to be led by your dreams and not pushed by your problems. That little saying will help you if you continue to focus on it. Lastly, just remember one other saying that I truly like. "The only difference between stumbling blocks and stepping stones is the way you use them."

Good luck to all you absolutely incredible kids!

Most sincerely,

Roy Williams

Roy Williams
Head Basketball Coach

ROY WILLIAMS
University of Kansas Head Basketball Coach, Lawrence, Kansas

KANSAS CITY ROYALS BASEBALL CLUB

Hi Kids,

Man, I don't know of a better time to be a kid than today! Just think of all the wonderful stuff that is at your disposal: science museums, libraries, amusement parks, swimming pools, the Internet, playgrounds, ball fields (not to mention the new "Star Wars" movie in May). However, it is up to you to take advantage of these awesome opportunities. America is the greatest country in the world, because it allows kids the chance to follow any dream they may have, no matter how big or small, and to make that dream come true.

Right now the world is like a huge menu and each of you can order whatever you want off of it. There is nothing that can't be accomplished through hard work, perseverance, patience, and a strong belief in yourself. Remember, the impossible is often the untried. Never let anyone tell you that you can't be what you want to be. It sure didn't stop the short basketball player or the tall jockey. Always keep your eyes on your goal so that you are not distracted by the stumbling blocks which may lay ahead of you. And if there are times when you might be a little discouraged or scared, just remember that there are plenty of people out there pulling for you: your parents, your teachers, your friends, me!

Finally, the most important thing that you can do as a kid doesn't take much time and doesn't cost any money, but you will be amazed by the results. Every night, give your mom and dad a kiss and tell them how much you love them.

Keep smiling,

Sluggerrr

Sluggerrr
Kansas City Royals

1985 WORLD CHAMPIONS • 1980 AMERICAN LEAGUE CHAMPIONS • 1976-1977-1978-1984 AMERICAN LEAGUE WESTERN DIVISION CHAMPIONS

SLUGGERRR
Mascot, Kansas City Royals

February 12, 1999

Dear Kids:

My name is Ken Canfield. I am the President and Founder
of the National Center for Fathering. I just wanted to take
a moment to let you know you are the reason for our work.
At the National Center, we're committed to encouraging
and equipping the men in your lives to become the best
fathers or father figures they can be!

We love kids. We know that you work hard every day
to learn and grow into young men and women who will
someday be moms and dads.

As kids, you have amazing potential to impact the world in
a way untouched by those in the past. As adults and parents,
we have failed in many ways to address the issues faced by
each of you. I believe that you will have the courage to stand
and face the trials and conflicts ahead.

We at the Center believe in each of you, and know that
you have what it takes to be whatever you aspire to be.
Have an Absolutely Incredible Day.

Sincerely,

Ken R. Canfield, Ph.D.
Founder and President
The National Center for Fathering

:-)

YAHOO!™

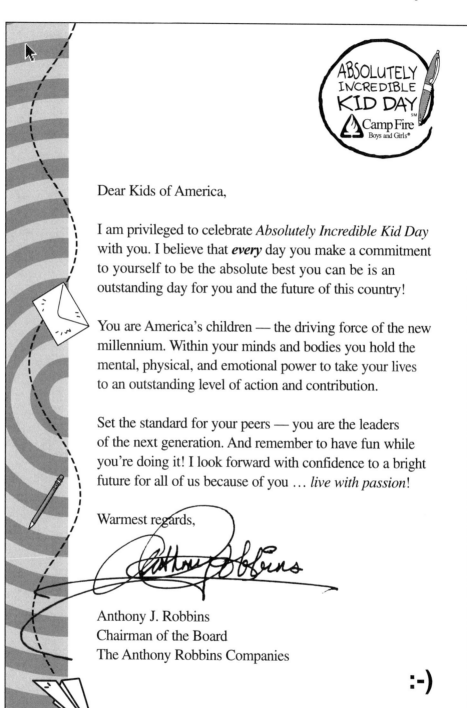

Dear Kids of America,

I am privileged to celebrate *Absolutely Incredible Kid Day* with you. I believe that *every* day you make a commitment to yourself to be the absolute best you can be is an outstanding day for you and the future of this country!

You are America's children — the driving force of the new millennium. Within your minds and bodies you hold the mental, physical, and emotional power to take your lives to an outstanding level of action and contribution.

Set the standard for your peers — you are the leaders of the next generation. And remember to have fun while you're doing it! I look forward with confidence to a bright future for all of us because of you ... *live with passion!*

Warmest regards,

Anthony J. Robbins
Chairman of the Board
The Anthony Robbins Companies

SOUTHWEST AIRLINES CO.

Herbert D. Kelleher
Chairman of The Board,
President & Chief Executive Officer

January 18, 1999

MEMORANDUM

TO: The Incredible Kids of America

FROM: Herb Kelleher

RE: Your Special Day

I think every day should be **Absolutely Incredible Kid Day**, because all kids are absolutely incredible. You bring fresh energy, curiosity, talent, laughter, and the excitement of learning to everything you do.

Someday, you and your young friends will be the ones who fly our airplanes and help our Customers. You will be the parents, doctors, nurses, teachers, business leaders, sports heroes, Congress members, authors, and scientists of tomorrow. So, even though every day is not called "*Absolutely Incredible Kid Day*," every day is important to you, and **you are a very important person.** You are in charge of the future!

Do as well as you can in all that you do. The sports, hobbies, chores, and homework you do today will bring you happiness and success in the future. Enjoy them, work hard, and have fun in the process.

Best wishes,

Herb

Herbert D. Kelleher

HERBERT D. KELLEHER
Chairman of the Board, President & CEO, Southwest Airlines

JOHN GLENN

COMMITTEES:
- GOVERNMENTAL AFFAIRS
- ARMED SERVICES
- SELECT COMMITTEE ON INTELLIGENCE
- SPECIAL COMMITTEE ON AGING

United States Senate

WASHINGTON, DC 20510–3501

To the Boys and Girls of America
on *Absolutely Incredible Kid Day*!

Dear Children,

It is nearly spring and time for plants to sprout and flowers to bloom.
There are new friends to meet and all kinds of interesting things to do. In my
childhood, spring was the time of year that I looked forward to with anticipation
and delight but I never seemed to have enough time for all of the fun and
wonderful things that I wanted to do. And like other children, along with
fun came the responsibilities of chores and school work. I know at times
it seems like hard work just being a kid.

So, make sure that all of you take the time this spring to be a kid. Besides,
it's fun to be a kid; it's neat to be a kid; and most of all, we adults love it when
kids are being kids. Whether at school with your studies or at the park
on a swing, you can use your imagination to explore your dreams and
make every day a new and wonderful adventure in life.

My wife, Annie, and I are very proud of our nation's young people and we
encourage each and every one of you to make your childhood as exciting
and fun as possible, and with the confidence in knowing that you are
all absolutely incredible kids!

Sincerely,

John Glenn
United States Senate

SENATOR JOHN GLENN
Former astronaut, Former United States Senator (D-Ohio.)

CHRISTOPHER S. BOND
MISSOURI

United States Senate
WASHINGTON, DC

March 18, 1999

To America's Children:

This is Your Day! Just as we celebrate Mother's Day and Father's Day to show our parents how much we love and appreciate them, *Absolutely Incredible Kid Day* is for you.

I would like to honor you today by recognizing how uniquely special each and every one of you are. It is my hope that you will never doubt your parents' love for you and that you will never be discouraged from following your dreams.

I dreamed vividly and often as a child! I always wanted to travel the world and to have a job where I could help a lot of people. Today, I am living that dream as a United States Senator for the State of Missouri. In my job, I have had the opportunity to travel to fascinating places like Southeast Asia, Europe and Mexico. I have also been deeply rewarded by passing laws and working to make life better for families in Missouri and across the nation.

My wish for each of you is that you will know the warmth of a loving family and that you will always have the encouragement and imagination to chase your dreams.

Sincerely yours,

Christopher S. "Kit" Bond

SENATOR CHRISTOPHER S. "KIT" BOND
United States Senator (R-Missouri)

UNITED STATES SENATE
WASHINGTON, D.C. 20510

KAY BAILEY HUTCHISON
TEXAS

To all our *Absolutely Incredible Kids*:

I would like to tell you just how *Absolutely Incredible* you are! Most likely, we have never met, but I wanted to share this day with you to let you know that I am thinking about you while I work.

As a United States Senator, my days are usually very long and I travel often in the State of Texas and to Washington D.C. Very often, my job takes me out of the country where I visit with world leaders. Together, we work on world peace, trade and other issues affecting your future.

Because you are *Absolutely Incredible*, I work to make certain the laws we create in the U.S. Senate are going to make this world safer for you, the water and air cleaner, and your education the very best.

My best advice to you: take the time each week to read an incredibly good book.

Sincerely,

Kay Bailey Hutchison

SENATOR KAY BAILEY HUTCHISON
United States Senator (R-Texas)

CITY OF AMARILLO

KEL SELIGER
MAYOR

To the Absolutely Incredible Kids of Amarillo:

It is a great honor for me to participate in today's festivities. Since I have two of you at home, I am constantly reminded of the enthusiasm, creativity, and affection that you bring to the lives of your families and to this city. I would like to share with you a lesson that I learned when I was a kid, although I don't know that I was nearly as incredible as many of you are. That lesson is that any job, endeavor, or project that is worth doing, is worth doing the very best that you can. I believe that this is the key to success at your age, and mine.

Every member of the City Commission joins me in celebrating your importance to our city. For you are the future leaders, builders, and citizens of Amarillo, and it will be your talent and dedication that will ensure that your city has the absolutely incredible future that you deserve.

Sincerely,

Kel Seliger
Mayor

MAYOR KEL SELIGER
Mayor, Amarillo, Texas

Office of the First Lady
Linda K. Graves

The Children of Kansas
Kansas Communities Across the State
Kansas, USA

Dear Children:

Today we celebrate Camp Fire Boys and Girls' *Absolutely Incredible Kid Day*, a day when grown-ups are reminded to write a letter to a child they know. While I don't know each of you personally, I feel like I know you. One of the privileges of being married to the Governor is getting to hear about many things going on in communities across our state.

Because today's children will be the leaders of tomorrow, I pay special attention to things I hear about Kansas kids. I hear about classrooms who have made commitments to improve their reading skills, students who have signed pledges to stay away from drugs, children who are helping others in their communities by collecting food and money for the hungry and kids who are promoting safety by always wearing their seat belts in the car. I can tell you, the children of Kansas are doing some pretty amazing things to make their homes, schools and communities a better, safer place to live.

You may not think you are making a difference, but you are. By taking responsibility for yourself, trying to do your best and working hard at school, you are setting a good example for other kids and that alone is really important.

Let me ask you to do just one thing for me: raise your hand in the air, reach over your opposite shoulder and pat yourself on the back. You are doing a great job!

Sincerely,

Linda K. Graves
First Lady

FIRST LADY LINDA K. GRAVES
First Lady, State of Kansas

Office of Mayor
Kathryn A. Yeager

October 14, 1999

From the Office of Mayor K♥y Ye♥ger,

I'd like to join the Camp Fire Boys & Girls Club in wishing every child in Wichita Falls a very special day on this ABSOLUTELY INCREDIBLE KID DAY!

I write this letter because I want you to know that <u>you</u> are an absolutely incredible kid! Every day you wake up in a world that is changing right in front of you...you accept the good times and learn to excel in the bad times that may come.

I admire how you can bounce back and try even harder every time something gets in your way. I can't resist how funny you are and the way your eyes light up when you tell another one of your jokes. It amazes me just how very beautiful you are and how you are going to touch the world in your own special way. It makes me feel proud to know that our fine city has so much because it has you in it.

So, every day, laugh a little more and try a little harder to be the best you can be...cause you're an ABSOLUTELY INCREDIBLE KID!

MAYOR

MAYOR KAY YEAGER
Mayor, Wichita Falls, Texas

Encouragement
From the Experts

E xperts say letter writing builds self-confidence!

Since Camp Fire Boys and Girls began planning *Absolutely Incredible Kid Day* in 1996, many child and family experts have provided guidance on how letter writing can have a positive impact on the life of a child. Some experts told us about a special letter that made a difference to them at a young age. Over the years, many of them who are speakers, authors and public figures have helped build excitement for this letter-writing campaign by endorsing and supporting Camp Fire's efforts. Others have offered suggestions and hints to help you write to the absolutely incredible kids in your life and community. Here, some of the most distinguished advisers in their fields encourage you to make letter writing a rich experience for both adult and child.

THE MESSAGE OF A LETTER

Gregory Jantz, Ph.D., *counselor; speaker; author,*
Becoming Strong Again: How to Regain Emotional Health

Hard to tell when something is priceless, just by looking at it. Just about a page, single-spaced, written on a leftover piece of notebook paper. Maybe with even a word or two misspelled, crossed out, rewritten. Page folded over twice, haphazardly or stuffed into an oversized envelope.

Somehow in our fast-paced, high-tech world, many adults have dropped the habit of writing letters. We call on the phone and leave messages on voice mail, but we don't write letters much. Even getting the mail, for adults, can be an annoyance. We receive so many pieces of mail daily, and mostly from people we don't know, or a bill we don't know if we can pay. A letter cuts through the clutter and says something important, that someone knows where to find us.

With children, getting a letter is recognition. Children receive birthday cards, holiday greetings, barely readable missives from future Hemingways in their third-grade classes, and exotic chain-letter requests from cousins in another state. Or, they get the latest toy they ordered off the back of a cereal box.

For children, letters have potential. Write knowing the letter will be tucked next to the heart of the child forever. It tells the child, "You are important to me."

WRITE LETTERS THAT ARE DEMONSTRATIVE. Explain the feelings you may or may not express openly. Avoid instructions that revolve around the child's behavior. A letter is a wonderful way to reinforce the value of the child's being, instead of merely the correctness of that behavior.

WRITE LETTERS THAT ARE DELIBERATE. Letters allow us to take time to craft the content of our message without sounding reactionary and immediate. Don't react to the circumstance, but to the enduring and endearing relationship we have with the child. With careful thought, we can construct each sentence, choosing just the right word or phrase to connect with the heart of that child.

WRITE LETTERS THAT ARE DURABLE. In a disposable culture, few things survive. If it's broken, we throw it out. If it's used up, we replace it. If it's forgotten for a while, we put it in a garage sale. Adults tend to want to replace old, worn-out things. Children often find those things the most comforting of all. Letters can be comforting to children because of their durability. They act as visual, tactile proof of your message. A letter can be taken out and reread as a reinforcement of the feelings it contains and a reminder of the relationship it represents.

EASE PEER PRESSURE WITH LOVE AND LOGIC®
By Dr. Charles Fay, *Cline/Fay Love and Logic® Institute*

What's a parent to do or say when their kids start "hanging out" with friends who remind them more of a horror show than the sweet little pals everyone had hoped his or her child would choose? Peer pressure is stronger than ever. Many kids are faced with life-and-death decisions about drugs, alcohol, sex and violence, starting as early as elementary school.

Out of great love for their children, some parents take the "bulldozer" approach to this problem. They rev up their engines, make a lot of noise and smoke, and try to overpower their kids. "Stay away from that Tommy! He's bad news! He's going to get you in a world of trouble!"

Every time kids hear this lecture, they interpret it as, "You're a wimp. You are so weak that you can't chose good friends and think for yourself when they want you to do something that is wrong!" Sadly, the parent-child relationship is wounded, and the child is now forced to make poor decisions in order to "win" the battle.

Other parents take a completely different tactic. These parents try to show their love by staying completely away from sensitive issues such as peer pressure, drugs, alcohol, violence and sex. "Kid, I don't care enough about you to be involved in your life," is the unintentional, yet very powerful, message sent by this strategy. Children and teens really do need and want us to be involved in these issues, despite their protests!

What's a loving parent to do? Develop practical ideas for staying involved in your child's life, and teach responsibility without creating power struggles and hurt feelings.

TRY SOME OF THESE IDEAS:
1. Don't forbid. The fastest way to get kids to spend more time with friends we don't like is to forbid them from doing so.
2. Send "You are Strong" messages, such as: "Your friends are lucky to have someone like you who can show them how to make smart choices."
3. Help kids take the pressure out of saying "no" by giving them permission to say, "No way. Last time I did that, my parents really let me have it."
4. Encourage responsibility by saying, "We know you are the kind of kid who is strong enough to live with the consequences of your choices."
5. Send plenty of unconditional "I love you" messages. Show your kids how much you care by asking them who they are going to be with and where they are going.

Writing a letter to your child about peer pressure is an excellent way to to "get the ball rolling" in a healthy way.

REVEAL YOURSELF IN A LETTER
By Lisa Marie Nelson, Ph.D.
broadcast journalist; co-author, The Healthy Family Handbook

Writing to a child is a wonderful way to express yourself. First, clarify your thoughts and put them on paper. Quickly jot a list of things that have happened and the way you felt about the child that made you smile. Your letter will be a keepsake that your child can keep to read and enjoy. It's also a great way for your children to get to know you. Keep these things in mind when composing your letter:

DO:
- Think of every letter as a love letter. Be kind and complimentary.
- Show interest in the reader's interests and activities.
- Remember names of pets, friends and schools.
- Offer encouragement and acceptance.
- Include tokens of friendship: stickers, coupons, confetti, photos, cartoons.
- Send the letter promptly so it doesn't get stale.

DON'T:
- Put anything in writing that you wouldn't want your own parents to read.
- Offer advice or criticism.
- Send articles like "How to Clear Up Acne" that show you want to change or "improve" the child's appearance or behavior.
- Go on and on about yourself and your awards and accomplishments. Leave the bragging to your parents.

POSTPONE ANYTHING BUT LOVE
By Ms. Randy Rolfe
author, The 7 Secrets of Successful Parents and You Can Postpone Anything But Love

WHEN YOU WRITE TO A CHILD, KEEP THREE GOALS IN MIND:
1. Build the child's self-image.
2. Build the child's sense of positive power.
3. Build their sense of power to contribute to the lives of others.

TRY THESE 10 WRITING TIPS TO HAVE A POSITIVE EFFECT
WHEN WRITING TO YOUR CHILD:
1. Use positive adjectives when describing the child. Your child faces plenty
   of demeaning or disrespectful words during the day. You show respect when
   you use these words: pleasing, capable, friendly, enjoyable, inspiring, wonderful,
   helpful, precious, thoughtful, beautiful, joyful, awesome, powerful, effective,
   attractive, knowledgeable, brilliant, valuable, fun, appreciative, handsome,
   fantastic, extraordinary, incredible.

2. Visualize positive futures for the child. Try a statement like this:
   "You are so good at … (exploring, running)."
   "You could be an … (astronaut, Olympic athlete)."

3. Show them how they please you.
   "I love it when you …"

4. Avoid using "shoulds." Instead, use your moral authority to praise what
   is good in them. TRY THIS:
   "I love seeing you …(clean your room on weekends, take a rest when
   you get tired, take care of a friend when they are hurting)."

5. Encourage them to communicate.
   "I love hearing you talk about your … (trip to the ball park, favorite video game,
   grandfather's jokes)."

6. Share the best of your own childhood. Reveal experiences you really enjoyed
   or remember fondly. Don't write to impress or amaze but to identify with
   the child's growth years. Write about the time you caught a butterfly and
   kept it alive for a few days. Or tell about the first time you rode a horse.

7. Validate intergenerational communication by showing what it means to you.
   "I remember when my mother (grandmother, aunt, teacher) …"

8. Ask about their life experiences in a way that expects a response. "What do you like best about school? Which teacher makes you feel like you want to go to that class? What's the funniest thing that happened to you and your best friend?" Questions like these help get your children emotionally committed and invested in their activities. It affirms that their feelings and desires matter, rather than pushing for results to please others. It shows your confidence that their gifts will emerge if they follow their own passion.

9. Share special interests you and your child have in common. Talk about swimming together, gardening, playing computer games, learning dog breeds, watching sci-fi movies, reading nature books, shopping, mixing fruit salad, or playing pop CDs.

10. Open and close with unusual, but positive, greetings. Never open with questions that ask for simple yes-or-no answers. You might write, "Dear, dear Jessica," or "To the one and only Robert." Don't close with advice or reminders. Close with confident well wishes. "I know you will have a great spring. You're the kind of person who knows how to live healthy and happy."

A LETTER OF KINDNESS AND DIRECTION
By Myrna B. Shure, Ph.D.
author, Raising a Thinking Preteen and Raising a Thinking Child

When I was a freshman in college and 17 years old, my mother was dying of cancer. My aunt wrote me a letter that helped prepare me for the inevitable. Her letter, both empathetic and factual, helped to focus not on the end, but on our life together. It helped me remember the wonderful moments, and how much my mother meant to me.

My aunt's letter helped me recall the good times and the bad, like when I got rejected from a girls' club in high school, and how Mom helped me get through that. She also reminded me of Mom's joy and support when I was voted into a sorority in college, which meant so much to me. I didn't know it then, but when Mom celebrated that sorority vote with me, she already knew of her diagnosis. She wouldn't spoil my moment.

My aunt explained that I should remember Mom for the kind of person she was and not dwell on any feelings of guilt for things I wish I had done or said. My aunt also wanted me to appreciate who my mother was.

That letter stayed with me for a long time. Mom died when I was 18. Whenever I felt overwhelmed by her loss, I thought of my aunt's letter to me. I'm 62 now. That letter stayed with me and comforted me all these years.

About Camp Fire Boys and Girls

Camp Fire Boys and Girls' mission is to build caring, confident youth and future leaders. One of those leaders is Kara Unruh.

When Kara was just 20 years old, she told her friends and family she wanted to help traumatized children confined in a Kosovar refugee camp. Kara's friends surely must have worried about her safety. But, in May 1999, she traveled to Albania and spent two weeks helping distribute 35,000 trauma care kits filled with treats and letters to soothe children needing medical attention. She organized games and led children in group activities to help take the edge off their confinement.

"My background in Camp Fire prepared me in so many ways for this trip," Kara says. "Camp Fire gave me the leadership skills I needed to get me through each day. They taught me to handle situations I know I'll encounter in my life."

There are 630,000 children and youth in 125 councils in 41 states and the District of Columbia who have similar experiences and lessons as Kara had in Camp Fire. They developed life skills, confidence, leadership skills and close friendships through a variety of experiences in Camp Fire Boys and Girls.

Kara, a member of Camp Fire for 15 years, has also attained the highest honor in Camp Fire, the Wohelo (WOrk/HEalth/LOve) Award. Each year, several hundred youth work hard and learn new skills as they, too, achieve this goal of the prestigious Wohelo Award. Some of the responsibilities Kara tackled to earn this award included volunteering at camp, working on the council's newsletter and chairing a Teens in Action committee. Now, at age 21, Kara serves as an AmeriCorps Promise Fellow for the Orca Council of Camp Fire in Tacoma, Wash.

Kids build confidence and practice leadership in Camp Fire. They learn how to give and receive support; they become leaders with positive influences; and they learn to give care and receive love from their families and friends. And because Camp Fire seeks opportunities to participate in the community, peers and community leaders value the kids.

Take Zach Newbrough, for example. Once considered an "at risk" kid, he now has a zest for life, largely due to summers at Camp Hantesa in Des Moines, Iowa, owned and operated by Heart of the Hawkeye Council of Camp Fire in Des Moines. At camp, Zach built a positive identity and learned to sail, rope climb and rappel down rock cliffs. His times in the "wild" have given him a strong sense of self-confidence and pride, strengths he'd like to pass along to others. Zach's new goal is to become a counselor and share his enthusiasm with younger kids, and he is in training with Camp Hantesa's Leadership Challenge program.

Zach is one of 2,500 youths ages 6 to 18 who attend the council's resident camp each summer. Boys like Zach make up 46 percent of Camp Fire Boys and Girls' membership. Nationwide, he's joined by more than 60,000 children who attend Camp Fire resident and day camps each year. Trained counselors do all they can to make sure kids leave camp with great memories, good friends and the confidence to succeed in school and life.

At first glance, "Camp Fire Boys and Girls" may seem centered around outdoor skills such as pitching a tent or learning basic survival skills. In truth, for 90 years, Camp Fire has worked with kids from kindergarten through college to help them develop social competencies, enhance problem-solving skills, and build positive, strong identities with a sense of their own power. Camp Fire aims to give kids a sense of purpose, worth and promise. That begins by providing a safe environment in which to learn and explore.

In addition to resident and day camps, Camp Fire Boys and Girls has other year-round youth development programs that are tailored to meet the needs of each community. Trained staff and volunteers use carefully constructed and well-researched national curricula to lead children and youth through programs that encourage exploration and build character. Camp Fire Boys and Girls is inclusive, welcoming children, youth and adults regardless of race, religion, socioeconomic status, disability, sexual orientation or other aspect of diversity.

Camp Fire Boys and Girls continually seeks leaders, volunteers and kids! If you are interested in getting involved, please call for more information. You can find Camp Fire on the Web at *www.campfire.org* or e-mail us at *info@campfire.org*. By phone, we can be reached at 816/756-1950. We'll keep the lines open for you.

Letter-Writing Kit: Start Now

Why Kids Love Your Letters

ids like to collect stuff. Rocks. CDs. Games. Notes from school.

Collections give them a reason to point to good times in their lives — times when the sky was blue, when money jingled in their pockets, when toys did everything they were told, and life was just plain good. Collections give children a reason to feel like they are in charge of the world.

A letter that makes it into that kind of collection is made of magic. The words of encouragement are so simple, yet so powerful that they would embarrass a child if the wrong person read them out loud.

Every parent can create a letter that lasts a lifetime. Begin with a pen or pencil and some paper, and let it be the link between your heart and your child. Afraid you'll cry? You might. But any time you touch the heart of another human being, you run the risk of getting your heart touched in return.

25 REASONS TO WRITE A LETTER NOW

1) Your son or daughter is offering to pay for a personal phone line.

2) A child solved a problem on your computer.

3) Your child just lost a baby tooth.

4) Your child learned how to count to 25.

5) A child just gave you a hug.

6) You heard a child sing in the choir.

7) A child is learning how to play a new instrument, and you recognized the song.

8) You want to celebrate a half-birthday.

9) A child helped you wash dishes.

10) A child learned how to sort clothes for the washing machine.

11) Your child kept the bedroom clean for two days.

12) A child showed kindness to another child.

13) Your child got 100 percent on a spelling test.

14) A young person righted a wrong.

15) Your child taste-tested a new vegetable.

16) You and a child saw a shooting star and talked about the power of wishes.

17) A child learned to sing the alphabet.

18) You remember how your child laughed after going to bed.

19) Your child had a great dental report.

20) A young person gave you great customer service.

21) A youth did more than you had asked.

22) The refrigerator door looks barren.

23) An adult child came home for the weekend.

24) An adult child gave you a surprise.

25) You're at work, and writing helps you remember a fond moment with your child.

10 TIPS FOR WRITING AN ABSOLUTELY INCREDIBLE KID DAY LETTER

1. Getting started can be the toughest part. Try "Do you know what I like about you? I like it when you ..."

2. Write what you mean, and make it from the heart.

3. Begin with a favorite poem or a famous quote that has special meaning to you.

4. Think of what you like best about letters that you've received.

5. Be specific and be descriptive. Use humor. Don't lecture.

6. Don't worry about the length. A note can be cherished as much as an epistle.

7. Write it by hand. Feel free to make edits as you go. Don't over edit.

8. Include things that you would like to hear in a letter that you might receive. Chances are, the incredible kid you're writing to feels the same!

9. Find time to write another letter. Make it a habit.

10. Write a letter now!

ABSOLUTELY INCREDIBLE KID DAY℠
△ Camp Fire Boys and Girls®

:-)

ABSOLUTELY INCREDIBLE KID DAY ^{SM}

Camp Fire Boys and Girls®

WRITE A LETTER TO A CHILD

A LOVING, SUPPORTIVE LETTER CAN MAKE A DIFFERENCE IN THE LIFE OF YOUR CHILD, A GRANDCHILD, NIECE, NEPHEW, KID DOWN THE STREET OR IN A LOCAL HOSPITAL.

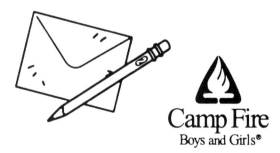

Camp Fire Boys and Girls®

Toll-free 1-888-2 KID DAY • E-mail: kidday@yahoo.com • Web site: www.campfire.org

Turn the page to get started!

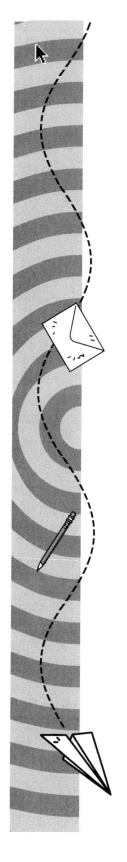

:-)

Camp Fire
Boys and Girls®

SOUTHWEST AIRLINES
A SYMBOL OF FREEDOM™

YAHOO!™

:-)

Camp Fire
Boys and Girls®

SOUTHWEST AIRLINES
A SYMBOL OF FREEDOM™

YAHOO!™

:-)

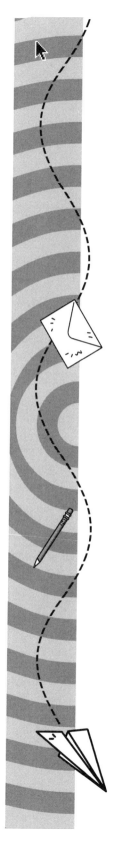

:-)

Camp Fire
Boys and Girls®

SOUTHWEST AIRLINES
A SYMBOL OF FREEDOM™

YAHOO!™

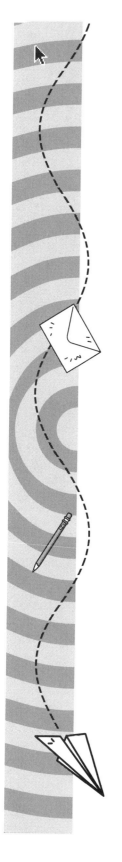

:-)

Camp Fire
Boys and Girls®

SOUTHWEST AIRLINES
A SYMBOL OF FREEDOM™

YAHOO!™

The Outdoor Book   (D-07600) $16.50
Find an adventure in your own back yard or explore the
wilderness on a hike or camp-out. This comprehensive
camping guide includes a program explanation and
many fun skills, activities, songs and recipes.

Wohelo: The Camp Fire History (D-27700) $6.95
Learn the history of Camp Fire Boys and Girls'
first years, from its founders to the inclusion of boys
and more.

Add $5.00 shipping and handling to any order.

Make checks and money orders payable to:
CAMP FIRE BOYS AND GIRLS
P.O. Box 804452
Kansas City, MO 64180-4452

To order call 1-800-669-6884, extension 286;
or contact us via e-mail, *customerservice@campfire.org.*